The USA
1917–1941

Ian Campbell

DUE

CAMBRIDGE
UNIVERSITY PRESS

PUBLISHED BY THE PRESS SYNDICATE OF THE UNIVERSITY OF CAMBRIDGE
The Pitt Building, Trumpington Street, Cambridge, United Kingdom

CAMBRIDGE UNIVERSITY PRESS
The Edinburgh Building, Cambridge CB2 2RU, UK
40 West 20th Street, New York, NY 10011–4211, USA
477 Williamstown Road, Port Melbourne, VIC 3207, Australia
Ruiz de Alarcón 13, 28014 Madrid, Spain
Dock House, The Waterfront, Cape Town 8001, South Africa

http://www.cambridge.org

First published 1998
Reprinted 2002

Printed in the United Kingdom at the University Press, Cambridge

Typefaces Monotype Octavian and FF Meta   *System* QuarkXPress®

A catalogue record for this book is available from the British Library

ISBN 0 521 56864 1 paperback

Produced by Gecko Limited, Bicester, Oxon

Illustrations by Gecko Limited, Bicester, Oxon

Picture research by Sandie Huskinson-Rolfe of PHOTOSEEKERS

ACKNOWLEDGEMENTS
Cover: Bridgeman Art Library.
Illustration from Harper's Bazaar; August 1930, The New Ford Roadster, Private Collection/Bridgeman Art
Library, London: p. 15b; Brown Brothers Stock Photos: pp. 12b, 14, 18b; Chicago Historical Society: p. 57l;
Library of Congress: p. 13; Corbis-Bettmann: pp. 4, 12t, 17, 25, 26t & b, 28, 30–31 background, 31tl, 39, 40, 41, 56;
Corbis-Bettmann/UPI: pp. 6, 23, 29, 42, 45, 46, 54, 58, 63–64 background; Franklin D. Roosevelt Library/Corbis:
p. 48; Getty Images: pp. 15–16 background, 20, 21, 22, 31b, 43, 51; The Ronald Grant Archive: p. 9; Famous
Players/Paramount (Courtesy Kobal): p. 18t; Peter Newark's American Pictures: pp. 51 & r, 11, 49t, 59;
Popperfoto: pp. 7, 19, 24l, 27, 36, 38, 61; Reproduced with permission of Punch Limited: p. 57r; Franklin D.
Roosevelt Library: pp. 49b, 53; Topham Picturepoint: pp. 10, 16t, 24r, 31br, 32, 35, 37, 44 background, 47, 50, 52,
55, 60, 62l & r, 64t.

We have been unable to trace the copyright for cartoons on pp. 33 and 34 and would be grateful for any
information that would enable us to do so.

Contents

America in 1917

America was the world's most prosperous nation in 1917. Standards of living were rising. America's industries were expanding. Large and efficient farms in the Mid-West grew vast quantities of cheap cereals that were exported to Europe. Americans had every reason to believe in a bright future for their nation.

America's attitude to the First World War

In 1914, war had broken out between the Central Powers (Germany, Austria-Hungary and, by 1915, Turkey) and the Allies (Britain, Russia, France and later Italy). The Democrat President of America, Woodrow Wilson, was anxious to keep America out of this conflict. Millions of immigrants, many originally from Europe, now lived in America. They had no wish to become involved in such a war. Most Americans hoped to remain apart from political and economic conflicts outside their own borders. This attitude became known as 'isolationism'.

America's isolationist attitude gradually began to change for a number of reasons.

The *Lusitania* incident

By 1915, Germany suspected that American ships were carrying ammunition to the Allies. As the Allies were blockading German ports, Germany felt justified in imposing her own 'war zone' around the British Isles. In February, she declared that her submarines would sink any enemy ship on sight, including any ships suspected of supplying war materials. On 7 May, the British Cunard liner, *Lusitania*, travelling from New York, was sunk by a German U-boat. Within twenty minutes, 1,198 civilians were dead. Among them were 128 Americans.

President Wilson immediately sent a strong protest to Berlin. Germany alleged that the *Lusitania* had been carrying ammunition but promised not to attack passenger shipping again without warning. America, therefore, stayed out of the war for the time being.

SOURCE A

A view of New York City's skyline from Brooklyn bridge in the 1920s.

After the sinking of the *Lusitania*, relations between Germany and America gradually grew worse. Early in 1917, Kaiser Wilhelm ordered that the policy of unrestricted submarine attacks against shipping should begin again 'with the utmost energy'. On 12 and 19 March, four unarmed US ships were sunk by German U-boats, and American public opinion turned even more sharply against Germany.

The Zimmermann Telegram

In January 1917, the German foreign minister, Alfred Zimmermann, sent a telegram to the German ambassador in Mexico. The telegram was intercepted by British intelligence and passed on to Wilson. It revealed that Germany had been trying to gain Mexican support in the event of war. In return for this, Mexico would be given the opportunity to invade America and seize Texas, New Mexico and Arizona. Americans were outraged. It was then discovered that German immigrants had been carrying out acts of sabotage in American factories and anti-German feeling grew even stronger.

America enters the war

On 6 April 1917, the American Congress declared war on Germany. President Wilson said 'The world must be made safe for democracy.' His aim was not only to stop Germany's aggression, but also to destroy the autocratic system of government in Germany.

America's role in the war

America had not been entirely neutral between 1914 and 1917, for she continued to trade with the Allies. As a result, American industry and agriculture had prospered. American banks had lent the Allies money to buy American products at high rates of interest. By 1917, her troops were desperately needed. The Russian army was collapsing and French and British morale was low. In March 1918, the Germans launched the 'Ludendorf Offensive' on the Western Front. At first this was successful but, by November 1918, there were almost 1 million US troops on the front line. The German generals sued for peace. An agreement, the Armistice, was made to end the war and, on 11 November 1918, both sides stopped fighting.

SOURCE B

Recruiting posters urging young Americans to join the armed forces.

AMERICA'S CONTRIBUTION TO THE FIRST WORLD WAR

Number of men conscripted into the forces	5,000,000
Number of troops wounded	125,000
Number of troops killed in action	53,000
Cost of munitions provided by the USA	$22 million
Loans to the Allies	$10 million

How did America's involvement affect ordinary American civilians?

The Federal government grew more powerful during the war as it was given greater control over industry and agriculture. Espionage Acts, limiting the freedom of speech, were passed. This made it more difficult for people to speak out against the government.

President Wilson and the Versailles Peace Conference

President Wilson went to the Versailles Peace Conference in December 1918, determined to find a 'just peace'. He issued his Fourteen Points, in January 1918, summing up his aims. The key point was a proposal to set up an international body, the League of Nations, to settle disputes between nations and prevent wars in future. At the Peace Conference, however, the other major nations – France, Britain and Italy – were mainly concerned with making Germany pay for the damage caused by the war. The Versailles Treaty that was finally imposed upon the Germans contained only a few of Wilson's Fourteen Points. The League of Nations was, however, included in the Treaty.

America returns to isolationism

When the Treaty was presented to the US Congress, to Wilson's intense disappointment it was rejected. The Republicans were concerned that America should keep complete control of her foreign policy and not become involved in the affairs of other nations. The most powerful nation in the world refused to take part in the League or enforce the peace treaty which their own President had helped to create. America had returned to isolationism.

Discussion points

> What were the main reasons for America entering the First World War?

> What is meant by isolationism?

SOURCE C

Ex-President Wilson (left) and his Republican successor, Warren Harding, riding to the Capitol from the White House. The occasion was Harding's inauguration as President in 1921.

The American success story

In the 1920s, the American economy was the most prosperous in the world. Electricity had arrived, and was gradually installed in homes, shops, offices, bars, motels and factories. New inventions, such as the refrigerator, radio, vacuum cleaner and, above all, the motor car, meant that the American economy prospered.

In what ways did America boom?

Henry Ford and mass production

The biggest industrial success of the boom years was the motor car. By 1925, millions of cars were being driven on America's roads, and their price was falling. How was all of this achieved?

The 'Tin Lizzie'

Henry Ford, the son of poor European immigrants, announced that he would 'build a car for the great multitudes'. In 1908, he made his first Model T Ford or the 'Tin Lizzie'. It was ugly, slow, uncomfortable, difficult to drive, and it rattled. But the Model T was tough, reliable, and it could travel anywhere. Most important of all – it was cheap, and became even cheaper. Between 1909 and 1928, 15 million Model T Fords were sold.

The role of the assembly line and division of labour

Henry Ford was able to produce his cars so cheaply because of the new industrial methods used in his factories. The key to success was division of labour. Each worker did just one task. For example, one worker would work a handle to stamp out hundreds of pieces of metal. The next man would drill the holes, the third man would bolt the pieces together. A moving assembly line was needed to make this process work.

SOURCE A

Henry Ford describes the assembly line:

Work is planned on the drawing board and the operations sub-divided so that each man and each machine only do one thing. The thing is to take the work to the man, not the man to the work.

Henry Ford, 1925

Henry Ford was using this assembly-line method to mass-produce the Model T by 1913. Before this, it had taken 12 hours and 28 minutes to manufacture one car. By splitting the job into 45 separate processes, manufacturing time was now cut to 1 hour and 33 minutes. By the mid-1920s, 7,500 cars were being produced a day – one car every 10 seconds. By 1929, 9 out of 10 US families owned a car made by either Ford, Chrysler or General Motors.

SOURCE B

Henry Ford and his son Edsel in 1924, with the ten-millionth Ford car to come off the production line.

THE EFFECTS OF THE MOTOR CAR

Positive effects

> The popularity of the motor car was a huge boost to other industries that produced the materials needed in its manufacture.

> New jobs were created to service the motor industry in building roads, constructing parking lots, manufacturing road signs and traffic lights.
Cars needed to be repaired and serviced and supplied with fuel. Gas stations, motels and restaurants sprang up all over America.

> The motor car was ideal for short-distance, convenience travel. Suburbs quickly expanded.

> Millions of families could now travel longer distances and take holidays.

Negative effects

> The car was a hazard to the environment: it caused traffic jams and air pollution.

> The car caused road casualties and deaths.

> Car assembly lines resulted in tedious and monotonous jobs with little job satisfaction.

> Some of the older generation felt that young couples were using the car for improper behaviour.

> Gangsters were able to use the motor car for their criminal activities.

PRICE OF A MODEL T FORD

1909	$950
1913	$600
1917	$360
1928	$290

THE VALUE OF CAR SALES IN THE USA

1920	US $1,800,000
1922	US $2,300,000
1925	US $3,800,000
1929	US $4,700,000

CARS ON THE ROADS IN THE USA

1910	468,000
1920	9,239,000
1930	26,750,000

DEMANDS CREATED BY THE MOTOR CAR

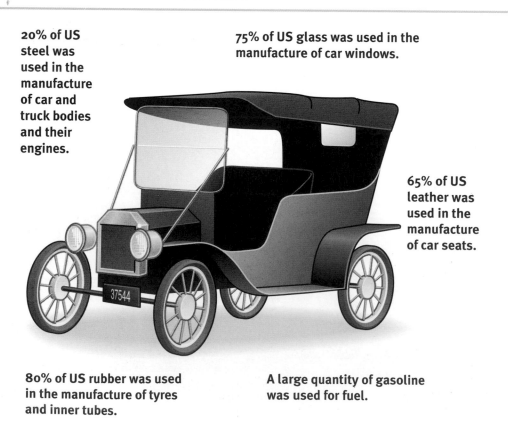

20% of US steel was used in the manufacture of car and truck bodies and their engines.

75% of US glass was used in the manufacture of car windows.

65% of US leather was used in the manufacture of car seats.

80% of US rubber was used in the manufacture of tyres and inner tubes.

A large quantity of gasoline was used for fuel.

The spread of automation

Mass-production methods soon spread to industries producing household electrical goods. Factories that had been making arms during the First World War were now geared up to produce the new labour-saving devices. By the end of the 1920s, radios, vacuum cleaners, refrigerators, irons and washing machines were all being produced in vast quantities. Because people were able to get access to credit and hire purchase more easily, sales of these items soon ran into millions.

SOURCE C

A scene from the popular film, Modern Times, *of 1936 showing Charlie Chaplin making fun of the tedious, boring work on an assembly line.*

SOURCE D

A recent historical study shows the extent of mass consumption in the American home.

The revolution was most apparent in the home. The percentage of households with inside flush lavatories rose from 20 to 51% between 1920 and 1930. Homes with radios rose from 0 to 40%; homes with vacuum cleaners from 9 to 30%; homes with washing machines from 8 to 24%.

Sean Cashman, *America in the 1920s and 1930s,* 1989

THE CONSUMPTION OF ELECTRIC POWER

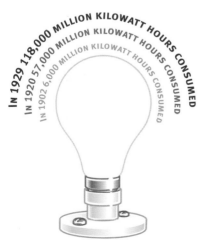

IN 1929 118,000 MILLION KILOWATT HOURS CONSUMED
IN 1920 57,000 MILLION KILOWATT HOURS CONSUMED
IN 1902 6,000 MILLION KILOWATT HOURS CONSUMED

By 1920, 33% of homes were supplied with electricity. By 1929, the proportion of homes with electricity had risen to nearly 70%.

The radio revolution

A new industry that completely captured the imagination of the American people in the 1920s was the radio or wireless. This device was developed before the First World War, but commercial production did not begin until 1919. This created thousands of new jobs.

The first broadcasting station, KDKA, opened in Pittsburgh in November 1920. It was privately owned, and received its income from advertisements on air. By 1940, there were over 700 radio stations all over America.

People listened to the new jazz music, sportscasts, news reports, political conventions, and sponsors' messages and advertisements. By 1929, 9 million American homes had a radio receiver.

HOW DID THE RADIO INDUSTRY AFFECT SOCIETY?

> The radio industry provided many new jobs.

> A new advertising medium was created.

> The radio helped to spread the popularity of the new dance and jazz music of the Roaring Twenties.

> The radio became influential in the spread of political ideas. President Roosevelt was the first politician to really understand the power of the new medium. He was to make very effective use of the wireless for his 'fireside chats' to the American people.

>> Activity

1 In what ways did American industry expand in the 1920s?

2 What were the most important reasons for the success of the motor industry?

3 How did the motor car provide a boost to other industries?

4 Explain how mass production helped in the new industries making electrical goods.

5 Why did the radio industry grow so rapidly? What influence did the radio have on American society?

Poverty in America

In a 1928 Republican election leaflet, Herbert Hoover promised 'A car in every garage, a chicken in every pot'. But this did not come true for every American.

Who did not benefit from the industrial boom?

America in the 1920s was, for some, a land of great opportunity and wealth. People talked of 'America the Golden' and the 'Land of Unlimited Possibilities'. But millions of Americans did not live in this comfortable world.

Because life during the economic boom was so exciting for some people, it is easy to imagine that all Americans shared in the wealth that was created. However, America was a divided society. There were a few very rich people at the top of society and many better-off Americans in the middle, but a large number living in poverty at the 'bottom of the heap'.

Who shared in the profits from industry?

The new industries made great profits, but there is little evidence that this wealth was shared out equally. The Brookings Survey of 1929 found that 18 million people lived in real poverty, and that 78 per cent of the profits from industry went to just 0.3 per cent of the population. By 1929, the average hourly rate of most production workers had risen by only 8 per cent since 1921.

Wages were higher for many skilled workers in the new industries. These were the Americans who could afford the motor cars and the new luxury gadgets. From 1921 to 1929, they saw their wages rise by as much as 35–40 per cent.

SHARE OF INCOME RECEIVED BY THE RICHEST 5% OF THE AMERICAN POPULATION

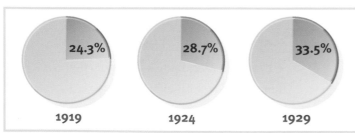

24.3% 1919

28.7% 1924

33.5% 1929

SOURCE A

This cartoon from 1928 shows the despair of the unemployed at Christmas.

Industries in decline

Workers actually lost their jobs in some areas of industry. In the textile and clothing industry, for example, new synthetic fibres like rayon were introduced and became very popular. They were produced in up-to-date, efficient factories that needed fewer workers. The old textile industries, like cotton, declined.

Coalmining and shipbuilding were not touched by the new technical revolution that boosted the manufacture of electrical goods and the motor car. Areas in America where these older industries had grown up – like New England and the South – saw very little industrial development.

AVERAGE HOURLY WAGES FOR FACTORY WORKERS

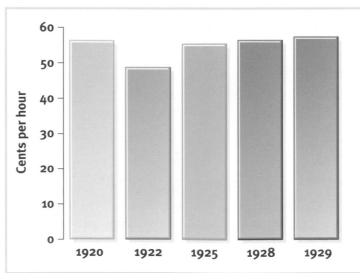

Trade Unions

As the big corporations became more efficient, they often cut down on their workforce. Management gained more power over employees because jobs were difficult to get. Large, efficient corporations were also able to take over many smaller companies who were competing against them. By the mid-1920s, the large corporations in the new industries, like the Ford Motor Company, were rich and powerful. Often, these big corporations were able to agree amongst themselves to fix prices at a certain level in a particular industry .

Very few workers belonged to a trade union. The big corporations, like Ford and General Motors, neither liked nor trusted unions. They thought that, if workers felt that they were badly paid, then it was up to them to improve their pay through individual negotiation. On the whole, the American public seemed to agree. Trade unions seemed 'un-American' to many people. Only the American Federation of Labour (AFL) had any power, and this union only represented the 10 per cent of the workforce who were skilled workers.

SOURCE B

This modern historian suggests that just a few corporations held huge power.

In the decade following the war, 1,200 mergers swallowed up more than 6,000 previously independent companies and, by 1929, some 200 corporations controlled almost half of American industry.

T. H. Watkins, *The Great Depression,* 1993

Underprivileged groups in society

Blacks

The poorest families of all were blacks who lived in the Southern states like Alabama, Louisiana and Mississippi. Most were descendants of former slaves, or ex-slaves themselves. They lived in rural slums and worked long hours on the cotton and tobacco plantations where the pay was very low. Some made a living as sharecroppers. Most whites saw them as inferior and they suffered severe discrimination in every area of daily life.

Many blacks migrated from these parts to northern cities like New York and Chicago. They lived in poverty in run-down districts, or ghettos, of the northern cities, like the Bronx or Harlem in New York.

SOURCE C

An overcrowded Negro shack in Virginia – blacks were the poorest of all the underprivileged groups in American society.

Immigrants

By the early 1920s, millions of immigrants from all over the world were living in America. Many were poorly educated, worked for very low wages and suffered from increasing prejudice. In particular, immigrants like the Puerto Ricans, Italians and Irish lived deprived lives in the ghettos of the major cities.

Many white, 'native born' Americans became more and more resentful of these new arrivals.

LAWS PASSED BY CONGRESS RESTRICTING IMMIGRATION

1917: A literacy test had to be taken by all prospective immigrants before they could enter America.

1921: A 'quota' system was set up. This limited the number of immigrants allowed to enter America each year to a certain figure, according to their country of origin.

1924: This figure was reduced still further. For the first time the numbers of Europeans entering America were limited.

1927: The quota of immigrants from Europe was reduced to 150,000 a year.

1933: Only about 23,000 immigrants were entering America each year.

IMMIGRANTS ENTERING THE USA EACH YEAR

Year	Number
1918	110,610
1920	430,000
1921	805,228
1924	706,896
1927	335,175
1930	241,700
1933	23,068

The government hoped that, if they did not interfere with the free market and competition, low prices, fair wages and high profits would follow. This policy was called 'laissez-faire', which means 'let things alone'.

The government did not, therefore, introduce a system of welfare or social security for the poor.

The 'laissez-faire' policy of the Republican government

The Republican presidents of the 1920s, Warren Harding, Calvin Coolidge and Herbert Hoover, believed in low taxes, high trade tariffs, and in helping big business as much as possible.

SOURCE D

Immigrants arriving in America around 1910.

>> Activity

1 Explain why some industries did not benefit from the boom.

2 Using all the information in this unit, explain what evidence you can find to support the following statements:

   a Many black people and immigrants had difficult lives.

   b Trade unions had limited power.

3 Why was there no system of welfare payments for the poor?

The plight of the American farmers

Agriculture during the First World War

During the war, demand from Europe for foodstuffs had soared. Encouraged by this, many farmers had borrowed heavily from the banks to buy new land and machinery. At first, this seemed very sensible. Europeans needed to buy American food, and they had the money to do so. When the war ended, however, European farmers began to re-build their own agricultural industry. American produce was no longer needed.

Farmers' problems after the First World War

During the 1920s, there was a huge surplus of food in the USA. Prices fell, and thousands of farmers desperately tried to solve their problems by borrowing more money from banks. From 1921 to 1929, they borrowed around $2,000 million. Rents and mortgages increased by over 30 per cent, so more and more farmers went out of business. By 1924, 600,000 were bankrupt and over 1 million farm workers had left the land.

FALLING PRICES IN THE 1920S

	1920	1932
Wheat	$1.82 (45p) a bushel	38 cents (10p) a bushel
Maize	61 cents (15p) a bushel	32 cents (8p) a bushel
Cotton	16 cents (4p) a pound	6 cents (1.5p) a pound

1 bushel = a dry measure of 8 gallons = approx 36 litres
1 pound = 0.454 kg

By the end of the 1920s, millions of farmers and farm workers were without work. Many expressed their anger and desperation by protests – particularly in the Mid-West. They demanded government action to raise farm prices.

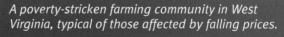
A poverty-stricken farming community in West Virginia, typical of those affected by falling prices.

FACTORS WORKING AGAINST THE FARMERS

> From the early 1920s, synthetic fibres like rayon were produced by the big textile companies. This meant less work for the cotton farmers.

> European countries could buy cheaper food from Canada, Russia and Argentina.

> American trade tariffs stopped foreign countries exporting manufactured goods to the United States. As a result, they had fewer US dollars with which to buy American wheat and cotton.

> Smaller farmers could not compete with the large planting corporations who could afford to use modern machinery.

> The US population fell, so there were fewer mouths to feed.

> The boom in the motor car trade affected the farmer. More cars meant less demand for horse fodder.

> More people were now consuming fruit, vegetables and milk, and less bread and meat. This made things worse for most farmers, whose chief products were wheat and cattle.

> Many of the poorer farmers went to the cities looking for work. Thousands ended up as 'hoboes' (tramps), living rough on the streets.

Unemployed farmworkers looking for work.

What did the Republican government do to help?

The government was reluctant to interfere with the 'free market'. However, some moves were made to help the farming industry.

> It was made easier for farmers to borrow money.

> Tariffs were increased still further against foreign imports. There were five increases between 1920 and 1930.

> Research was commissioned into the causes of pests and droughts.

Unfortunately, none of these actions made any real difference to the farmers' problems.

Discussion point

> Look through all the information in this unit. Do you think anyone was to blame for the poverty of the American farmers?

America's economic success

THE KEY FACTORS IN AMERICA'S ECONOMIC SUCCESS

> The American government did not interfere in business; reduced taxes and abolished many regulations.

> The American economy benefited from the First World War. Large amounts of money were available for investment.

> America was rich in natural resources such as oil and fertile land.

> American industry was protected by trade tariffs which kept out foreign goods.

> Advertising and marketing were used effectively to sell the new products.

> The growth of credit and hire purchase gave a boost to the new industries.

> New methods of manufacture, for example mass production, meant that consumer items could be produced cheaply and in large numbers.

THE BOOMING INDUSTRIES

The two vital elements in the economic boom were the arrival of electricity and mass production.

The new industries

> The motor car industry led the way to mass production and division of labour.

> The motor car industry needed vast quantities of steel, rubber, glass, oil and fuel. New restaurants, motels and gas stations sprang up all over America. New roads and towns were developed. The car also brought with it pollution, traffic jams, road casualties and monotonous jobs on the assembly lines.

> The new electric consumer industries all used the mass production principle. By the mid-1920s, hundreds of factories were producing electrical goods for the home. Credit enabled consumers to buy.

> The radio industry captured the imagination of the public. It was used extensively by the big corporations to promote their new products. By 1929, 9 million homes had a radio.

An advertisement from Harper's Bazaar, *in August 1930, for the new Ford Roadster motor car.*

Which industries did not benefit?

The traditional textile and clothing industries suffered as more and more clothing was made from synthetic materials in modern factories. Coalmining and shipbuilding also went into decline.

WHO LOST OUT?

> Immigrants

> The poor and unemployed

> Blacks

> Farmers

Children playing in their tenement homes in a rundown inner-city area.

WHY DID AMERICAN FARMERS NOT SHARE IN THE PROSPERITY?

> After the First World War, demand in Europe for American farm products fell.

> A falling population meant fewer mouths to feed.

> New synthetics, like rayon, were replacing cotton.

> Cheaper agricultural products came in from Canada and Argentina.

> High tariffs prevented foreign countries from buying US goods.

> Large planting corporations put small farmers out of business.

> The popularity of the motor car meant less need for horse fodder.

> Changed eating habits meant less demand for meat and bread.

> The government offered little help. Tariffs were introduced on foreign agricultural imports and the farmers were offered loans.

THE ATTITUDE OF THE REPUBLICAN PRESIDENTS

All three presidents of the 1920s had similar views on how the USA should be governed.

> Harding coined the phrase: 'back to normalcy'. Like many Americans, he wanted to turn away from Europe and concentrate on allowing American business and industry as much freedom as possible.

> Coolidge invented the slogan 'the business of America is business'. He held the same views on business and government as Harding. Taxes were kept low and tariffs high.

> Hoover was a firm believer in 'laissez-faire' and 'rugged individualism'. He believed that the government should not interfere in business.

Old and new in America

The new wealth created by the economic boom meant that many Americans were able to follow a new, more exciting lifestyle. As a result, American society changed a great deal in the 1920s.

What were the main features of the Roaring Twenties?

Social conflict

Not all Americans approved of these changes in society. Some, especially the older generation, supported Prohibition — the banning of alcohol — and were strongly opposed to the social changes of the 1920s. Because their views were so different from the new generation of young Americans, it was a time of great social tension.

SOURCE A

A novelist of that time wrote:

The parties were bigger – the pace was faster – the shows were broader, the buildings were higher, the morals were looser and the liquor was cheaper.

F. Scott Fitzgerald, *Tales of the Jazz Age,* 1922

SOURCE B

Bessie Smith, the blues singer.

The jazz age

Music played a big part in the social revolution of the Roaring Twenties. Blues music had originated in the southern states of America like Mississippi and Alabama. The blues were one way in which black slaves could express their misery and hardship. The songs were accompanied by cheap, simple instruments like the guitar, banjo and harmonica. Before long, this music had reached the streets, the dance halls and the Mississippi steamboats. Singers like Fats Waller and Bessie Smith introduced their blues songs to city audiences in the new clubs and speakeasies. Jazz, which developed from ragtime and the blues, was the most popular new music of the 1920s. By the early 1920s, jazz had reached Chicago. It found a home in the bars and speakeasies, where flappers and their slick-haired partners danced to the irresistible beat of the new music.

The early gramophone record companies and first radio stations took advantage of this new commercial opportunity, and jazz became more and more popular throughout the 1920s and 1930s.

Popular dances

To accompany the jazz music of the clubs, new kinds of dances soon came into fashion. The most famous dance of all was the Charleston, originating from a club in Charleston, Carolina. Many of the older generation were shocked by what they considered to be the 'loose morals' of the young.

SOURCE C

A religious newspaper of the time commented:

The music is sensuous, the embracing of partners is absolutely indecent; and the motions – they are such as may not be described in a family newspaper.

The Catholic Telegraph, 1925

Short-lived fads

People embraced many new and short-lived fads and crazes. Many businessmen were prepared to invest in new and unusual schemes. There were a variety of beauty contests, dance marathons, stunt flying exhibitions, even live goldfish-eating competitions. There were crazes for board games like 'mah-jong' from China, and simple crossword puzzles became fashionable. Perhaps strangest of all, however, was a man called Shipwreck Kelly who sat on top of a flagpole for an unbelievable 23 days and 7 hours. Others tried to beat this record, but none succeeded.

Big-time sport

Sport flourished in the Roaring Twenties. Many Americans now had more leisure time and money to spend. The new commercial radio stations brought sports news into every home, and helped to create a new generation of heroes, like the golfer Bobby Jones and the boxer Jack Dempsey.

The Hollywood film industry

The most glamorous aspect of the Roaring Twenties was the film industry. The very first moving pictures consisted of images projected onto a screen by a machine called a 'kinetoscope'.

SOURCE D

Shipwreck Kelly on top of his flagpole.

SOURCE E

A poster advertising Rudolf Valentino in The Sheik.

Its inventor, Thomas Edison, believed, at first, that it would just be a passing craze, confined to fairgrounds and music halls. By 1929, 110 million people were going to the cinema each week.

The first film actors were silent, anonymous figures with names like 'The man with the sad eyes'. Then, in 1909, a famous producer, Carl Laemmle, decided to promote Flo Lawrence as a star in one of his films. Almost immediately, the public reacted with great enthusiasm, and the star system was born. Movie bosses realised that the 'star appeal' was more important than the story itself. Warner Brothers, Paramount, MGM, and the other big studios, organised their publicity departments to produce 'material' on the new stars which would interest the public. When Rudolf Valentino died in 1926, aged only 31, crowds queued for hours to see his embalmed body.

The Hollywood success story

The film studios were attracted to Hollywood, a suburb of Los Angeles, because it had clean air, a sunny climate and it was close to mountain and desert scenery.

Here, the studios made Westerns, crime films, religious epics and slapstick comedy. Sentimental stories with children and animals were particularly successful.

In 1927, *The Jazz Singer*, the first ever 'talkie' was made. In it, Al Jolson spoke for the first time on screen, and the film industry was revolutionised.

SOURCE F

This historian suggests that Hollywood worked like a factory:

On the whole, Hollywood films of the 1920s were custom
made according to very tired formulas. Conformity and
repetition ensured mass production as regular as that of any
other factory.

Sean Cashman, *America in the 1920s and 1930s*, 1989

The new mass media

A clear record of the changes in attitude that resulted from the
Roaring Twenties can be found in the leading magazines of that
time. Many new titles, like *Life, Vogue* and *Harper's Bazaar,* were
introduced catering for the tastes and fashions of the day.

A passion for heroes? – the story of Charles Lindbergh

Lindbergh was a young aircraft pilot who took up the challenge
offered by a New York businessman to fly non-stop from New York
to Paris for $25,000. On 20 May 1927, he took off from Roosevelt
Field, New York, in a single-engine monoplane, *The Spirit of St
Louis.* He had no radio, no map and no parachute – just a few
sandwiches, two pints of water and an inflatable raft.

The whole adventure captured the imagination of the American
public. When the news came that he had arrived safely at Le
Bourget, near Paris, after a flight of 3,600 miles (5,760 kilometres),
people reacted with pride and enthusiasm. The *New York Times'*
headline read: 'Lindy does it – to Paris in 33.5 hours'.

When Lindbergh returned home, huge crowds watched the welcome
parade in New York. Over 1,800 tonnes of ticker tape were thrown
from office windows in celebration. 'Lucky Lindy' personified the
ultimate 'American Dream'. He was rugged, tough, self-reliant and
brave – all the legendary American qualities in one.

SOURCE G

Charles Lindbergh standing in front of his plane,
The Spirit of St Louis.

>> Activity

1 How did young people spend their leisure time
   in the 1920s?

2 How did Charles Lindbergh symbolise the
   spirit of the times?

3 Why did some older people disapprove of young
   people's behaviour?

Racial intolerance

One group of Americans who preached intolerance and spread fear in the 1920s was the Ku Klux Klan (KKK). Many people from the southern states joined this secret society, believing that they were standing up for traditional American values. In fact, they were supporting an organisation that stood for religious and racial hatred.

How widespread was racial intolerance in the 1920s?

The origins of the Ku Klux Klan

The original Klan was formed as a friendly club in 1866 by ex-Confederate (Southern) troops after the Civil War. The name came from 'kyklos' – the Greek word for circle. It was soon discovered that the robes, hoods and rituals of the club terrified black people in the South, only recently freed from slavery. This fact appealed to racist whites. Soon, many similar, secret groups had formed, and the Klan became a focus for violence against black people. However, by 1869, the overall leader – the Grand Wizard – decided to disband the KKK, because the violence had grown extreme and out of control.

In 1915, the Klan was re-formed by a teacher of Southern history called William Simmons. The Klan was now opposed to Jews, Catholics, radicals, socialists, and all foreigners. In particular, Klan members hated blacks. Strict segregation laws, separating blacks from whites, had been imposed in the southern states in the early 1900s, but many blacks had new hopes and aspirations after the ending of the First World War.

SOURCE A

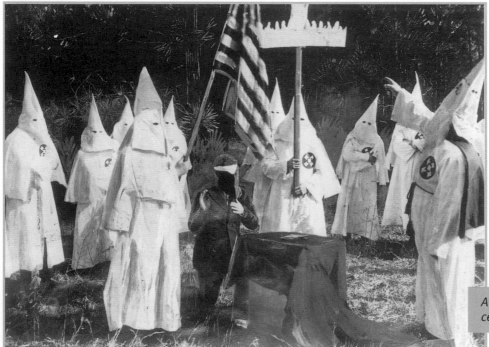

SOURCE B

Extracts from the Kloran (Klan book of rules):

Are you a native born, white, gentile American?

Do you believe in and will you faithfully strive for the eternal maintenance of white supremacy?

What kind of people joined the Klan?

In the early 1920s, a fund-raiser called Ed Clarke started to recruit members in a very businesslike way, appealing to a variety of prejudices. He employed sympathisers to recruit new members for $10, $4 of which they kept for themselves. By 1924, Klan membership had risen to 4 million.

In 1923, a dentist called Wesley Evans took over from Clarke. Under his leadership, the Klan moved into local state politics. Judges, local officials and policemen all became members. Local politicians and businessmen sometimes supported the KKK for political reasons and were often too frightened to offend the Klan in any way.

A new member is initiated at a Klan ceremony in November 1922.

SOURCE C

One writer said:

Literally half the town belonged to the Klan when I was a boy. At its peak, which was from 1923 through 1925, the Nathan Hale Den had about five thousand members, out of an able bodied adult population of ten thousand. With this strength the Klan was able to dominate local politics.

Robert Coughlan, *Konklave in Kokomo*, 1949

Most supporters of the KKK were ignorant, southern whites, who believed that they were defending the American way of life against all kinds of enemies. The rituals and mystery brought a kind of purpose and excitement into their lives.

SOURCE D

Lyrics of an anti-racist song written for the black singer, Billie Holliday:

Southern trees bear a strange fruit, blood on the leaves, blood on the root,
Black bodies swinging in the southern breeze,
Strange fruit hanging from the poplar trees,
Here is a fruit for the crows to pluck,
For the rain to gather, for the wind to suck
For the sun to rot,
For the tree to drop
Here is a strange and bitter crop.

Levis Allen, 1939

A lynch mob and their victims in the deep south during the 1920s. The term 'white trash' was used by more educated Americans to describe the kind of people in the photograph.

SOURCE E

A modern author ridicules the KKK:

Rural fear of urban foreigners gave rise to a resurgence of the KKK, a collection of bigots who hated 'race-mixing', Jews, Catholics in equal proportions. They struck fear into the hearts of anyone who did not fit the organisation's definition of a 'true American'.

T. H. Watkins, *The Great Depression*, 1993

The decline of support for the Klan

In 1925, the Klan was involved in scandal by the 'Grandest Dragon' of the Klan, D. C. Stephenson. He was found guilty of the rape and mutilation of a woman on a Chicago train. The public were outraged and the Klan went into decline. By 1930, only scattered cells of die-hards were left but racism did not cease to exist.

>> Activity

1 Why was the Ku Klux Klan so powerful for a short time during the 1920s?

2 Why did the Klan lose its support towards the end of the 1920s?

Religious intolerance

After the First World War, many conservative Americans wanted to rekindle old, traditional values. They turned to a fundamentalist form of Christianity which teaches that every word in the Bible is literally true.

What form did religious intolerance take?

Fundamentalists bitterly attacked Charles Darwin's Theory of Evolution, which appeared in his book *On the Origin of Species*. Darwin argued that life on earth began millions of years ago, and that all living things had evolved by natural selection. This horrified the fundamentalists. They argued that God created the world in six days.

Fundamentalists set up the Anti-Evolution League in 1924, and persuaded several states to ban the use of Darwin's book in schools.

Johnny Scopes challenges the law

The Civil Liberties Union in New York offered to support anyone who would test this law. A young Tennessee teacher, Johnny Scopes, let one of his friends file a law suit against him for teaching the Theory of Evolution. The Civil Liberties Union took up the case and took on the famous liberal lawyer, Clarence Darrow, to defend Scopes. The prosecution lawyer was William Bryan, a committed fundamentalist, who had once run for President. The case aroused international interest and, for eight days in July 1925, the eyes of America and the world were on the town of Dayton, Tennessee which had a population of only 6,000. It was the first trial to be broadcast on the radio.

SOURCE B

A fundamentalist view:

We cannot have a system of education that destroys the religious faith of our children.

William Bryan, 13 May 1925

The 'Monkey Trial'

Soon, Dayton was swarming with hot dog and lemonade stands, circus sideshows and various revivalist preachers. The courtroom was packed with over 1,000 people from the first day on 10 July 1925. The trial itself turned into a farce and many of the anti-evolutionist arguments were seen to be foolish. However, the jury found Scopes guilty and he was fined $100. A year later, the Tennessee Supreme Court overruled the Dayton judgement. Several states kept this law on the statute book until the 1960s and 1970s although it was never applied again.

SOURCE A

Anti-evolution books had a record sale in Dayton while Johnny Scopes' trial took place.

>> Activity

1 How did the 'Monkey Trial' show the tension or conflict between traditional and modern in the 1920s?

2 Why did the Civil Liberties Union decide to challenge the fundamentalists?

3 Why did the 'Monkey Trial' become an international event?

The Red Scare

In the 1920s, millions of Americans were benefiting from the economic boom. Consequently, people who criticised American society were thought to be unpatriotic or 'un-American'.

How widespread was political intolerance in the 1920s?

Many Americans in the 1920s feared two groups in particular. One group was the anarchists, who believed that there should be no government or laws in society. The other was the communists, who believed that the state should control all factories.

Communism and capitalism

The suspicion of communists or 'reds' in America went back to the Russian Revolution of 1917. The new communist government had taken over all private fortunes, industry and land. In 1919, their leader, Lenin, set up an organisation called Comintern, dedicated to the spread of world communism. The American system is based on capitalism, which allows individuals to do what they like with their money. Under communism, society as a whole is more important than the individual. To Americans, communism was a deadly disease to be feared and hated. This was in spite of the fact that only about 0.1 per cent of the population belonged to communist or anarchist groups.

The Palmer raids

One man who particularly hated communism was A. Mitchell Palmer, the US Attorney-General. In the summer of 1919, a small group of radicals bombed his house. The 'reds' were blamed and, on New Year's Day 1920, Palmer ordered raids on the homes of suspected communists and anarchists. Over 6,000 people were arrested, most of them immigrants. No evidence could be found, yet many were jailed and some were deported. Finally, in May 1920, the raids were called off.

Why was there so little protest?

Despite the fact that 6,000 people had been wrongly arrested, there was little protest against Palmer's actions. Fear of communism meant that most Americans kept quiet.

SOURCE A

Mitchell Palmer's house in Washington after it was bombed by a group of radicals.

The Sacco and Vanzetti case

The Red Scare reached a climax with the trial and execution of Nicola Sacco and Bartolomeo Vanzetti. On 5 May 1920, these two men were arrested and charged with carrying out a payroll robbery that ended in the deaths of a guard and paymaster. From the outset, public opinion was against them because they were immigrants and anarchists. They had also left America during the First World War to avoid being conscripted into the armed forces.

SOURCE B

Vanzetti was clear about why he was being punished:

I am suffering because I am a radical, and indeed I am a radical; I have suffered because I was an Italian, and indeed I am an Italian.

Bartolomeo Vanzetti, 1921

The evidence against them was flimsy. Both men had guns on them when arrested in Massachusetts. The bullets in Sacco's gun were said by the police to be the same size as the ones which killed the guard. But many respectable Americans carried firearms. Although 61 eye witnesses of the wages robbery identified Sacco and Vanzetti, the defence produced 107 witnesses who swore to seeing them at another place. Yet the jury found them guilty, and Sacco and Vanzetti were sentenced to death. Shortly after, Judge Thayer was heard to say: 'Did you see what I did to those anarchistic bastards the other day?'

SOURCE C

Sacco and Vanzetti manacled together after hearing that they had lost their appeal. It was now 1926 and they had already spent five years in prison.

A miscarriage of justice?

The case aroused a great deal of concern in America and in other countries. In Paris, a mob attacked the American embassy.

Even though a confessed murderer, Celestino Madeiros, admitted to the crime, the two Italians lost all appeals. On 23 August 1927, they were executed in the electric chair.

SOURCE D

A German cartoon shows Sacco and Vanzetti looking to the electric chair for salvation rather than to American justice.

Fifty years later, the State Governor of Massachusetts, in the presence of Sacco's grandson, acknowledged that the trial had been a miscarriage of justice.

>> Activity

1 Why did many Americans fear the spread of communism?

2 What happened to Sacco and Vanzetti?

Prohibition and the gangsters

In October 1919, the American Congress passed the Eighteenth Amendment to the Constitution. This was a change in the law that led to the Prohibition, or banning of all alcohol, in the United States. It came into force on 16 January 1920, and remained until December 1933. The law stated that: 'the manufacture, sale or carriage of alcoholic liquors for beverage purposes is hereby prohibited'.

Why was Prohibition introduced in 1919, and then discarded in 1933?

The growth of the Temperance Movement

Since the 1830s, temperance societies had been demanding a ban on alcohol. These organisations argued that drinking led to ill-health, crime and poverty. The most powerful was the Anti-Saloon League (ASL), a group that issued pamphlets and advertisements, held meetings, and put pressure on politicians.

By 1919, many individual states had banned the sale of alcohol.

SOURCE A

Women in a saloon in Oakland, Indiana, during the 1880s, keeping a record of the men buying drinks. The women had tried to drive them out by bringing a skunk into the bar.

The effect of the First World War

During the First World War anti-German feeling had increased. The ASL took advantage of this by reminding the American people that German-born citizens owned and controlled the drinks trade.

SOURCE B

The British writer G. K. Chesterton summed up wartime feelings:

Prohibition was passed in a sort of feverish self-sacrifice and patriotism.

Prohibition becomes law

On the first day of Prohibition, in January 1920, the ASL wished everyone a 'Happy Dry Year'. They were convinced that it would do nothing but good for America.

Bootlegging

Bootlegging involved making or importing illegal alcohol, and selling it to eager customers ready to pay the going rate. Some alcohol came from Canada, some from the West Indies, some across the border from Mexico. 'Rumrunners', fleets of ships piled high with liquor, landed in quiet coves, and trucks carried their cargo to the city bars.

Many Americans made their own beer, wine and spirits and drank it at home. The government estimated that, in 1929, 700 million gallons of beer were produced in American homes, and that even children were regularly drinking home-made liquor.

SOURCE C

A popular rhyme from the 1920s:

Mother's in the kitchen, washing out the jugs,

Sister's in the pantry, bottling the suds,

Father's in the cellar, mixing the hops,

Johnny's on the front porch, watching for the cops.

Anon

The speakeasies

Americans who wanted a drink in town had no trouble getting one in any of the thousands of speakeasies, or illegal bars, that sprang up almost overnight. Before Prohibition, New York had 15,000 bars. By 1926, there were 30,000 speakeasies within the city. Anyone could get into the speakeasies provided they knew the password. Prices were high, and the quality of the alcohol varied a great deal. Sometimes alcohol known as 'Moonshine' was made in home-made stills, some of it doctored from industrial alcohol. About 5,000 people died from the effects of this bad liquor each year.

Al Capone and the gangsters

The era of Prohibition led directly to an increase in serious crime. Huge profits could be made from bootlegged liquor, and most of the speakeasies were quickly taken over by powerful gangs. These organisations also controlled the distilleries, and ruthlessly exterminated their rivals. The gangster, Al Capone, was responsible for over 500 murders during his infamous career. On 14 February 1929, Capone's henchmen, disguised as policemen, murdered seven members of the Bugs Moran gang. This became known as the 'Valentine's Day Massacre'.

SOURCE D

A speakeasy during Prohibition.

SOURCE E

The St Valentine's Day gangland murder in Chicago.

Chicago — a city of gangsters

Chicago became the most notorious of the gangster strongholds. It was here that Al Capone ruled over his vast empire based on the profits from the trafficking in illegal alcohol. He maintained his position by intimidation and bribery. Officials like Chicago mayor Big Bill Thompson and police chiefs were paid for their silence.

PROHIBITION IN CHICAGO

> In 1925, there were over 10,000 speakeasies in Chicago.

> In 1925, Chicago, with a population of 3 million, had 16,000 more arrests for drunkenness than the whole of England and Wales, with a population of 40 million.

> By 1927, deaths from alcohol were 600 per cent up on the 1920 level.

What did the authorities do to fight back against the gangsters?

The Prohibition Bureau was set up to deal with the problem but it had less than 2,000 agents and limited funds. The Bureau itself soon became involved in scandal and corruption.

From 1924, the Bureau of Investigation (later the FBI), was more successful. Led by J. Edgar Hoover and the 'G Men', the Bureau met the gangsters on their own ground, using tougher methods of enforcement. It was this agency that finally had Capone imprisoned in 1932 after he was convicted of tax evasion.

SOURCE F

Al Capone on a train to Atlanta Federal Penitentiary in 1934, after being convicted for Federal income tax evasion.

An impossible law to enforce?

By the end of the 1920s, it seemed that Prohibition had been a failure. Juries were unwilling to convict and the law difficult to enforce. Many Americans were regularly drinking alcohol, and a whole new world of crime had been created. America has 29,000 kilometres of coastline, making smuggling easy. People were making their own liquor, and industrial alcohol was easily diverted for private use.

SOURCE G

This modern historian states:

From Canada chiefly, but also from Mexico, liquor flowed across the borders in a deluge. It entered the States by railroad, truck, passenger vehicle, speedboats.

John Kobler, *Ardent Spirits: Rise and Fall of Prohibition*, 1993

ILLEGAL STILLS SEIZED BY THE POLICE AND AUTHORITIES

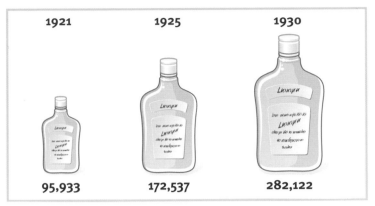

In 1929, President Hoover set up the Wickersham Committee to look at the state of the Prohibition Law. Their report admitted that the law was not working.

The effects of the Depression

The Depression finally killed off Prohibition. The 'wet' supporters argued that many new jobs would be created if the alcohol industry were to operate again.

Roosevelt and Hoover

In the 1932 Presidential campaign, Roosevelt and the Democrats were firmly against continuing Prohibition. Hoover and the Republicans more or less ignored the issue. They lost the election, and on 5 December 1933, Prohibition was finally abolished by the Twenty-first Amendment to the Constitution. One Congressman said: 'Let us flee from Prohibition as one would from a foul dungeon'. Millions of other Americans celebrated in style.

>> Activity

1 Why do you think the anti-alcohol campaigners were able to have Prohibition made law in 1919?

2 What was the impact of Prohibition in these areas:
   > law and order
   > social life
   > respect for the law?

3 Why did America eventually drop Prohibition in 1933?

The role of women

Before 1914 women had a lower status than men in society. Most important of all, they did not have the vote. The position of women began to change as a result of the First World War. The war offered women the opportunity to prove their skills and abilities, as they took over many jobs traditionally associated with men. In the 1920s, many American women, especially the younger ones, began to question values and attitudes that had previously been accepted.

How far did the role of women change during the 1920s?

VOTES FOR WOMEN

> In the early 1900s, Susan Anthony formed the International Women's Suffrage Alliance. This organisation campaigned for votes for women and joined with the British Suffragette Movement, whose leader was Emmeline Pankhurst.

> In 1912, Alice Paul and Lucy Burns formed the Congressional Union (later the National Women's Party). This called for a national amendment to the American Constitution that would give the vote to all American women.

> Women's rights campaigners fought to win the vote, state by state. By 1919, women could vote in 29 states.

> In 1920, the Nineteenth (Women's Suffrage) Amendment became part of the American Constitution. American women had won the right to vote.

Flappers and freedom

A number of young women, the so-called 'flappers' of the new generation, took advantage of their newly found freedom by smoking, wearing make-up and perfume, and going for all-night drives with their boyfriends. Some even admitted to drinking 'bootleg' liquor in speakeasies, and having sex before marriage.

SOURCE A

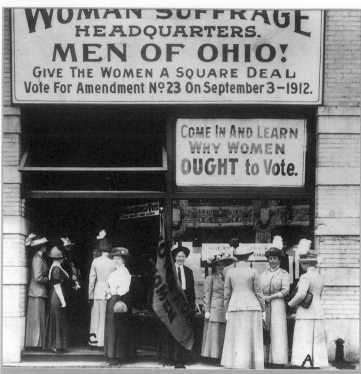

Suffragettes campaigning for the vote in Cleveland in 1912.

Many other Americans from the older generation were outraged by this kind of behaviour. In Chicago, women with short skirts and bare arms were liable to be fined between $10 and $100. American mothers formed the 'Anti-Flirt League' in an attempt to curtail the activities of the flappers – but they were fighting against the spirit of the times.

SOURCE B

A magazine article defends the changes in women's behaviour:

The older generation had pretty well ruined this world before passing it on to us – then they are surprised that we don't accept it with the same attitude as they did when they were young.

J. F. Carter, *Atlantic Monthly*, 1920

SOURCE C

A modern historian suggests that the increasing emergence of the flappers was closely tied up with the economic boom:

The flapper was a vital economic symbol. She could buy silk stockings, jazz records, or rouge compacts. Clothes, the great liberator, were her major hallmark.

Nancy Woloch, *Women and the American Experience*, 1996

SOURCE D

Flappers arrested in Chicago, in 1922, for wearing what were considered to be scanty bathing costumes. Special police were hired to make these arrests.

Members of the Anti-Flirt League were also outraged by the work of Margaret Sanger. She had been a nurse in New York's tenement district, where she became aware of the desperate situation faced by mothers with too many children and very little money. With great determination, she campaigned for the provision of birth control facilities for the poor. She lived to see over 200 Planned Parenthood clinics open throughout America.

A move towards feminism?

Mass production of household goods gave many women more time away from household chores. There were more opportunities for women who wanted to work and increase their independence.

Many turned their attention to the growing number of pressure groups, like the League of Women Voters, who were seeking more power and status for women in society. They had their own magazines, and discussed and supported issues like feminism and equality. Female writers and journalists, such as Dorothy Parker, also made their mark on society. In particular, magazines like *Judge* tried to appeal to the new 'liberated' woman of the 1920s, and the pursuits of pleasure. This led to criticism that some of these publications were too concerned with materialism and the 'good times'. But this did not stop them becoming tremendously popular.

Although men still held the real positions of power, women's expectations were changing.

SOURCE E

A feminist women's magazine stated:

Everyone will agree that the foundation of feminism is belief in women as human beings. Women were hampered throughout their lives by dozens of rules for respectable female behaviour.

Women's Leader, 1928

SOURCE F

A modern historian explains how women were able to raise their status:

Women virtually took over the occupations of librarian, nurse, elementary school teacher. By 1930, over 90 per cent of librarians were women. A larger proportion wanted salaries and promotion equal to men.

Stanley Cohen, *Rebellion against Victorianism,* 1991

>> Activity

How much did the role of women in America really change after the First World War?

America in the 1920s

WHAT WERE THE MAIN FEATURES OF THE ROARING TWENTIES?

> The popularity of jazz including the new music of Fats Waller, Bessie Smith and others.

> New dances and short-lived crazes.

> An increasing interest in sport. Golf, baseball, boxing, tennis, horse racing, basketball, all became multi-million dollar attractions in the 1920s.

> The growth of the film industry. By 1929, 110 million a week were going to the cinema.

> The emergence of the mass media. Magazines and radio catered for a new mass market.

> Figures like Charles Lindbergh, who personified Americans' hopes and aspirations, became popular heroes.

INTOLERANCE WITHIN AMERICAN SOCIETY

> Socialists, communists and anarchists were feared and hated. Over 6,000 people were arrested after a series of bomb outrages in the Palmer Raids of 1920. In 1920, following a payroll robbery, two Italian immigrants and anarchists, Sacco and Vanzetti, were falsely charged with armed robbery and murder. They were found guilty and executed in 1927.

> Fundamentalist Christianity gained in strength, especially in the Bible belt of the Mid-West. The 'Anti-Evolution League' did not approve of Charles Darwin's Theory of Evolution. Several states made it illegal for the theory to be taught in schools. In Tennessee, Johnny Scopes challenged the law on teaching evolution. He was prosecuted in the famous 'Monkey Trial'. Scopes was found guilty but the judgement was later reversed.

> Racial intolerance was widespread, especially in the southern states. The Ku Klux Klan was re-formed in 1915 by William Simmons. It was dedicated to upholding white supremacy. During the 1920s, the Klan were responsible for lynching many blacks who were innocent of any crime. There were nearly 4 million members by 1925. By 1930, membership of the Klan was in decline because of its involvement in scandal but racial violence lived on.

Prohibition and gangsters

Following pressure from temperance groups, the Prohibition of Alcohol Law was passed in 1919. The bootlegging industry was born and thousands of 'speakeasies' sprang up throughout America.

In Chicago, Al Capone built up a huge empire based on the profits from trafficking in illegal liquor and eliminated his rivals by intimidation and violence. He avoided prosecution until 1932. Even then, he could only be charged with tax evasion.

The Prohibition Law became almost impossible to enforce and eventually most Americans ignored the law.

Finally, in March 1933, Roosevelt's new government got rid of the Prohibition Law. Americans could once again drink legally, and the gangsters had to turn to other areas of crime to make their profits.

Contraband beer, tipped out of barrels, flowing down a street in the 1920s.

Prohibition agents examining some of the 3,000 bags of liquor hidden in a coal freighter in New York harbour.

WOMEN IN THE 1920s

> Flappers smoked, wore make-up, drank in speakeasies and sometimes had sex before marriage. They symbolised the new social attitudes of the times.

> Margaret Sanger was the best-known campaigner for birth control for the poor. She opened clinics throughout America, despite the opposition.

> Mass production of new electrical household goods gave women more leisure time and freedom.

> Pressure groups like 'League of Women Voters' came into being.

> There was a 'backlash' against these 'liberated women' from many of the older generation who were shocked by their behaviour.

How far did women's roles change before 1920?

Before 1917, women's campaigners had fought for women's rights and the vote. Society's attitude towards women changed during the First World War and, by 1920, American women had the same voting rights as men.

·LIFE·

G.PATRICK NELSON
PARIS 1911

LA MARQUISE CIGARETTES
of a "vintage"

LA MARQUISE
CIGARETTE
DE
QUALITE SURFINE

An advertisement for cigarettes aimed at women.

Causes and consequences of the Wall Street Crash

The Wall Street Crash, of October 1929, was the sudden, dramatic event that sparked off the Great Depression in America. Countless investors panicked and sold their shares overnight and hundreds of thousands of people were ruined.

Why did the economic boom of the 1920s end in such disaster in 1929?

In autumn 1928, President-elect Hoover announced: 'We, in America today, are nearer to the final triumph over poverty than ever before in the history of any land. The poor-house is vanishing from among us.' But the American economy was not as strong as it seemed.

The unequal distribution of wealth

By 1929, at least one-third of all income generated by the economy went to only 5 per cent of the American people. Many Americans, therefore, could not afford to buy a car, a radio or a refrigerator. The US economy had been built on the principle of mass production but the market for consumer goods was limited.

SOURCE A

A stockbroker's office in the 1920s. The clerks are chalking up the rising share prices.

Poor overseas markets

Foreign nations needed firstly to sell their goods to American firms in order to get the currency they needed to buy American goods. But the American government had imposed high tariffs against foreign goods. This made them too expensive. Therefore, these countries, in turn, imposed their own duties on American products. As a result, fewer and fewer American goods were sold abroad.

Too many goods and not enough demand

By 1929, therefore, the demand for goods produced by American factories was falling. Manufacturers started to cut back on production. By 1928, 2 million Americans were out of work.

Heavy borrowing

By the late 1920s, millions of Americans were in debt. Everyone was so confident in the future that companies, stockbrokers, speculators and private individuals all borrowed heavily from banks and financial institutions.

The Wall Street share boom

Throughout the Roaring Twenties, as company profits increased, buying stocks and shares was seen as a risk-free way of making money. This was the speculation game. Speculators invested in private companies. As soon as the share price had increased, they sold at a profit.

More and more ordinary Americans bought shares, sometimes investing their life savings.

SOURCE B

A historian writes:

By summer of 1929, stock prices had nearly quadrupled compared to four years earlier. Transactions ran to 5 million a day. Few held shares for income. What counted was the increase in capital values.

J. K. Galbraith, *The Great Wall Street Crash*, 1971

SOURCE C

The Director of General Motors wrote:

Suppose a man begins a regular savings of $8 a month. If he invests in common stocks, he will, after 20 years, have at least $80,000. Anyone can not only be rich, but ought to be rich.

John Jaskob, 1928

Buying on the margin

Owning shares was made even easier because they could be bought on credit. The stockbroker would accept a 10 per cent deposit called a 'margin'. With luck, the shares could be sold before the rest had to be paid. A big profit could be made for a very small investment.

Brokers took this risk because they were so confident that the prices of shares would keep on rising.

How long could the share boom last?

The share boom was at its peak from 1927 to 1929. Sometimes share prices fell, but buyers hoping for a bargain would buy up these shares and confidence in the market would return. But this system only worked as long as everybody was confident that share prices would go on rising.

The share bubble of speculation

While confidence remained, the share boom continued. By 1929, people from all sections of society – nurses, window cleaners, cowboys, film stars – all seemed to be playing the market. Billions of dollars of investment had inflated the price of shares way beyond their true value. Once confidence went, the share bubble of speculation would burst. If prices began to fall and stockbrokers and investors lost confidence they would want to sell their shares. Many banks had accepted shares as security for loans. If the value of the shares were to fall below the amount of the loan, the banks would demand repayment in cash.

THE US SHARE BOOM

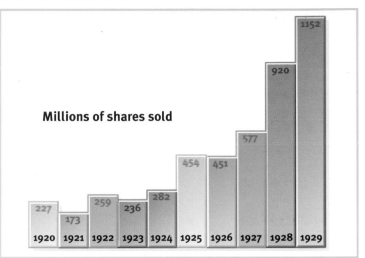

Millions of shares sold

1920	1921	1922	1923	1924	1925	1926	1927	1928	1929
227	173	259	236	282	454	451	577	920	1152

The Florida Land Boom, 1924–6

Easy credit also enabled people to speculate in property. The land boom was very similar to the share boom. Land was bought with a 10 per cent deposit (called a 'binder'), and then sold for a large profit.

An example of such a scheme occurred between 1924 and 1926. Estate agents described a number of building plots for sale in Florida in glowing terms, even though most of them were swampy and nowhere near the beach. But many Americans were attracted to the prospect of making money through buying land on the warm Florida shores and then selling it for a profit.

SOURCE D

INVESTOR—*Now, let's see, where did that agent say my lot was?*

A cartoonist makes fun of the Florida Land Boom.

The Florida Land Boom ends

For a while, prices rose rapidly, and many people did well. But then buyers started to realise that most of the deals were worthless. Prices plunged and many banks, builders and individuals went bankrupt.

Finally, in 1926, two hurricanes hit Florida, killing hundreds and flooding thousands of plots. The boom was over.

SOURCE E

A historian points to the attractions of the boom:

Some of the land sold in Florida was genuinely attractive: much of it was not. Roughly 90% of those buyers had no intention of ever occupying the property. The trick was to get out before the collapse.

Robert McElvaine, *The Great Depression, America 1929–41*, 1984

Could people see that a crash was coming?

By 1929, many people could see the problems which had arisen. Bankers had become aware of the risks involved and tried raising interest rates, hoping to put people 'off the margin'. But this did not have the desired effect.

SOURCE F

A writer remembers his feelings:

Everyone was playing the market. On my last day in New York I went to the barber. As he removed the sheet, he said: 'Buy Standard Gas. I've doubled. It's good for another double.' As I walked upstairs I reflected that if the hysteria had reached barber-level, something must soon happen.

Cecil Roberts, *The Bright Twenties*, 1938

SOURCE G

A financial expert stated:

Sooner or later, a crash is coming and it may be terrific.

Roger Babson, September 1929

>> Activity

1 What were the main reasons why, by 1929, American firms could not sell all their goods?

2 Why had people borrowed so heavily by 1929?

3 What happened during the Florida Boom?

4 Why do some historians point to the 'speculation game' as the most important factor in the Crash?

SOURCE H

'Say, Doc, do me a favor. Just keep your eye on Consolidated Can Common, and if she goes bearish tell my broker to sell and get four thousand shares of P & Q Rails Preferred on the usual margin. Thanks.'

This cartoonist suggests that the Wall Street boom has gone too far.

Boom turns to bust

By the summer of 1929, stocks of unsold goods were piling up in many factory warehouses. As a result, many investors began to sell their shares and rumours began to circulate that profits in industry were falling.

How did the Wall Street Crash come about?

Black Thursday

As investors continued to sell their shares, share prices continued to fall until, on 24 October 1929, panic hit Wall Street. As soon as the Wall Street gong was sounded at 10 a.m., the rush to sell began. In the 1920s, an average Wall Street day would involve trading of about 2–3 million shares: a busy day might see that figure rise to 5 million. On Black Thursday, nearly 13 million shares changed hands and millions more were offered for sale but did not find buyers.

Prices started to plunge. The news spread quickly throughout America, and more and more people instructed their brokers to sell.

The New York bankers intervene

On Black Thursday, six of the richest bankers in New York met to decide on a plan to calm the market and reassure the investors. They decided to send six banking officials to spend $240 million on a selection of shares – $40 million each. They hoped that this would restore confidence. For a while, the plan seemed to work. Prices were low, but they stopped falling.

The leader of the six bankers, Thomas Lamont, from Morgan's Bank, said: 'There has been a little distress selling on the stock exchange.'

SOURCE A

A reporter wrote:

They roared like lions. They hollered and screamed, clawed at one another's collars. It was a bunch of crazy men. Every once in a while, when shares in Radio or Steel took another tumble, you'd see some poor devil collapse and fall to the floor.

Stock Exchange Guardian, 1929

SOURCE B

An article in a newspaper reported:

Huge crowds surged up and down the narrow streets in search of excitement. Rumours were started. A trader, caught by the falling price of shares, jumped from a window. From then on, reports were frequent that brokers and others had jumped from windows.

New York Herald Tribune,
25 October 1929

SOURCE C

Investors anxiously waiting in Wall Street, on 29 October 1929, for the latest news.

Terrifying Tuesday

On Monday 28 October, the selling continued and 9 million shares were traded. But the worst day of all was Tuesday 29 October. Desperate investors and brokers were trying to raise cash to pay back loans to banks. Many of the shares bought by the bankers a few days earlier were now back on the market.

The teleprinters could not keep pace with the frantic activity. In one day, 16 million shares were sold. Hundreds of thousands of investors were ruined.

In the days and weeks that followed, prices continued to drop. By 13 November, they had hit their lowest levels. It was far too late to repair the damage done by the Crash.

PRICES OF SHARES IN CENTS

	3 September	13 November
Union Carbide	137	59
General Motors	182	36
Radio Corporation of America	505	28
Woolworths	251	52

The Wall Street Journal, 1929

SOURCE D

An eyewitness to these events, Arthur Robertson, said:

October 29th, 1929, yeah. A frenzy. Suicides, left and right. People I knew. It was heartbreaking. On Wall Street, the people walked around like zombies.

Studs Terkel, *Hard Times: An Oral History of the Depression*, 1986

SOURCE E

No one was responsible for the Wall Street Crash. Hundreds of thousands were driven to it by the lunacy which always seizes people who think they can become very rich.

J. K. Galbraith, *The Great Crash*, 1961

WALL STREET CRASH

23 October:	26 million shares sold at falling prices
24 October:	13 million shares sold
25 October:	Prices steadied at lower level
28 October:	Much heavier selling as prices fall steeply 9 million shares traded
29 October:	16 million shares offered for sale Average share price fell 40 points Shareholders lost $8,000 million
13 November:	Lowest share levels reached A slow recovery began Total losses amounted to $30–40,000 million

SOURCE F

An investor, who has lost everything, tries to sell his expensive car for only 100 dollars!

>> Activity

Study all the information in this unit and the previous unit on pages 32–34.

1 Explain the chief factors which led to such frantic selling from Black Thursday onwards.

2 What attempts were made to stop the panic? Why did they fail?

The Great Depression

The Wall Street Crash had severe and long-lasting consequences for America.

How did the Wall Street Crash affect America?

SOURCE A

The writer of these lyrics was moved by the plight of so many desperate people queuing in breadlines or begging for money or food.

They used to tell me I was building a dream
with peace and glory ahead
why should I be standing in line
just waiting for bread?
Once I built a railroad, made it run
made it race against time
once I built a railroad, now it's done
Brother can you spare a dime?

Yip Harburg, *Brother can you spare a dime?*, 1932

SOURCE B

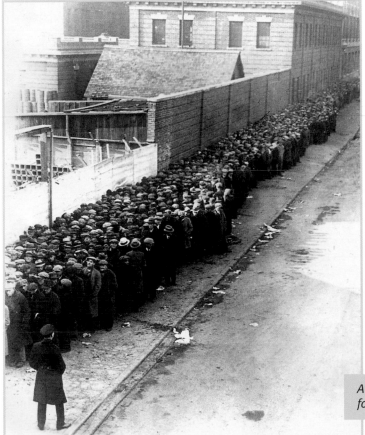

A long queue of unemployed men waiting for free food and assistance in New York.

The Wall Street Crash had a devastating effect on the US economy and that of the rest of the world. Only a small proportion of Americans actually owned shares – less than 1 per cent of the population. Yet the Crash affected the vast majority of the American people because there were serious weaknesses underlying the US economy.

Money for investment dried up. Workers lost their jobs as more companies went out of business. As unemployment rose, people had less money to spend. There was, therefore, less demand for products and more companies went under. This was known as 'the cycle of despair'.

COMPANIES GOING OUT OF BUSINESS (thousands)

1928	1929	1930	1931	1932	1933
109	104	122	133	154	100

NUMBERS OF UNEMPLOYED (millions)

1928	1929	1930	1931	1932	1933
1.5	2.3	4.3	8.0	12.0	12.8

UNEMPLOYMENT AS A PERCENTAGE OF THE LABOUR FORCE

1923	1930	1931	1932	1933	1934
3.2	8.7	15.8	23.6	24.9	26.7

The banks in crisis

As the effects of the Crash took a hold, millions of savers wanted their money back from the banks. But the banks had problems of their own. Many had lent unwisely to stockbrokers, unsound companies and private investors. When they called their debts in, many borrowers could not pay them back.

The smaller banks were the first to go bankrupt. Within three years, thousands of larger concerns had also failed. By 1933, the American banking system had virtually collapsed.

BANK FAILURES

1929	1930	1931	1933
642	1,345	2,298	over 4,000

The unemployed

By far the most tragic consequence of the Crash was widespread unemployment. This led to terrible poverty. All over America, crowds of shabbily dressed men without jobs – hoboes or tramps – walked the streets looking for work, or queued for hours for food at soup kitchens and in breadlines.

SOURCE C

At first, it was hoped that the situation might improve, as most of the big corporations had survived the Crash. But, as the Depression deepened, demand went down, and the jobless total reached enormous proportions. It was worst of all in the industrial cities. In Chicago, 40 per cent were out of work.

Who kept their jobs?

Most employers were slow to fire workers, and only did so when there was no alternative. But, gradually, more and more factories had to lay off workers, reduce wages and make other savings. Most of the 60 per cent of workers in Chicago who kept their jobs saw their wages cut by a half or more.

SOURCE D

One historian writes:

Writers who observed the large numbers of unemployed described the psychological effects of idleness in the same terms. George Orwell visited a family in a northern mining town [in England], all out of work: 'grown up sons and daughters sprawling about ... one tall son sitting by the fireplace too listless to notice the entry of a stranger, slowly pulling off a sticky sock from a bare foot'. The American historian, Ray Billington, interviewed scores of applicants. He later recalled their 'bleak, downcast eyes, their broken spirit'.

The writer Sherwood Anderson said: 'There is in the average American a profound humbleness. People seem to blame themselves.'

J. A. Garraty, *The Great Depression and the New Deal*, 1990

The unemployed queuing at Al Capone's soup kitchen in Chicago, in 1930.

Laissez-faire

SOURCE E

The American President said:

I am convinced we have now passed the worst and with continued unity of effort we shall rapidly recover.

Herbert Hoover, May 1930

SOURCE F

A prominent industrialist said:

The average man won't really do a day's work unless he is caught and can't get out of it. There is plenty of work to do – if people would do it.

Henry Ford, March 1931

The views expressed in Sources E and F represented the feelings of many Americans in the 1930s and reflected the attitude known as laissez-faire. This was the policy of President Hoover and the Republicans. Their belief that the government should not interfere in the economy meant that there were no unemployment benefits or welfare payments for the poor.

SOURCE G

Hoovervilles, hunger and shame

Over a million of the unemployed had become homeless because they could not pay their rents or mortgages. Banks had taken possession of their homes. Now they felt anger and humiliation and blamed President Hoover's government. They lived in shanty towns on the outskirts of cities. They built their new homes from packing cases, scrap metal, sacking, wood, perhaps an old car seat, and burnt old engine oil for warmth on a cold night. These settlements became known as 'Hoovervilles'. People got their food from rubbish tips, or queued for hours for free food at charity kitchens. Others simply begged on street corners. Many slept rough in doorways, parks and subways.

SOURCE H

A reporter wrote:

There is not a garbage dump in Chicago which is not diligently haunted by the hungry. Last summer in the hot weather when the smell was sickening and the flies were thick, there were a hundred people a day coming to one of the dumps. A widow fed herself and her 14-year-old son on garbage. Before she picked up the meat, she would always take off her glasses, so she couldn't see the maggots.

New Republic Magazine, February 1933

A typical home in a shanty town in New York during the 1930s.

SOURCE I

Peggy Terry, who lived through these times, later said:

In Oklahoma, people were living in old, rusted-out car bodies or in shacks made out of orange crates. One family with a whole lot of kids was living in a piano box. This wasn't just a little district, this was ten miles wide and long.

Studs Terkel, *Hard Times: An Oral History of the Depression*, 1986

SOURCE J

A novelist contrasted the plight of the poor with the New York skyscrapers:

The Woolworth building was not 50 yards away, a little farther down the silver spires and needles of Wall Street, great fortresses of stone and steel that housed enormous banks. There, in the cold moonlight only a few blocks away from this abyss of human misery, blazed the pinnacle of power where a large section of the entire world's wealth was locked away in mighty vaults.

Tom Wolfe, *Look Homeward Angel*, 1929

Black people during the Depression

Blacks were already the most deprived section in American society. Those who lived in the slums of the northern cities and in the farming areas of the South suffered terrible hardship. Unskilled workers suffered most of all.

SOURCE K

A member of the Teamsters' (truck drivers) Union said in an interview:

The Negro was born in depression. It didn't mean much to him: the Great Depression as you call it. The best he could be is a janitor or a porter or a shoeshine boy. The Great Depression only became official when it hit the white man.

Clifford Burke, early 1930s

The American farmers and the Depression

During the Depression, life became even harder for America's farmers. The farmers were producing too much food. While the poor starved in the cities, food rotted in the countryside. People in the towns could not afford to buy the farmers' produce.

Banks were not sympathetic. If farmers could not pay their mortgages, their land was re-possessed.

In farming states like Iowa, farmers joined together and tried to drive away the bailiffs who came to evict them with shotguns and pitchforks. The Farmers' Union organised strikes to stop food getting to the market – in the hope that prices would rise. They blocked roads, and marched through streets with placards announcing: 'In Hoover we trusted, now we are busted.'

SOURCE L

An impoverished family in a shack in Tennessee during the Depression.

The Bonus Army

One protest which did worry the Republican government was the Bonus Army March on Washington. In 1932, over 20,000 of the ex-servicemen who had fought for America in the First World War, decided to demand bonus payments that had been promised to them. This bonus of a few hundred dollars each was scheduled for payment in 1945. These veterans wanted their money now as many were facing starvation. Thousands of these Bonus Expeditionary Force (BEF) veterans marched on Washington from all over America. They set up a gigantic Hooverville opposite the White House on the Anacosta Flats.

US Congress did not vote to pay the bonus immediately but did vote money to help the veterans pay their way home. Most left, but between 2,000 and 4,000 remained. President Hoover and the government were disturbed by these 'troublesome veterans'. They declared that they were led by communists and revolutionaries. After two BEF men were killed in a clash with police, Hoover ordered the army to move them out. On 28 July 1932, four troops of cavalry drove the veterans out of Washington and burned their Hooverville camp. To many Americans, it seemed that this was a declaration of civil war by the government against its own people. Was America now close to revolution? The *New York Evening Post* described it as 'easily the most threatening situation the Depression has brought upon America'.

SOURCE N

A recent history book suggests that the American people did not have much sympathy for the Bonus Marchers:

Hoover's office had no flood of letters. There were no mass demonstrations. Hoover dismissed the BEF as 'thugs, hoodlums and communists'.

Louis Liebovich, *Bylines in Despair,* 1994

>> Activity

1 What were the factors which led to such high unemployment by 1933?

2 Why were the American banks unable to help industry?

3 Which groups were worst hit by the Great Depression?

4 What was the Bonus March crisis? Why did President Hoover order the marchers to be removed from Washington?

SOURCE M

Children in the Bonus Marchers' camp waiting for their fathers who were lobbying in Congress for payment of their bonus money.

The 1932 Presidential election

In November 1932, the American people went to the polls to vote for a new president. The Republican candidate, Herbert Hoover, had been President since 1929. The Democratic candidate was Franklin D. Roosevelt, Governor of New York State.

Why did Hoover lose and Roosevelt win?

When the Depression began in 1929, President Hoover and the Republicans tried to reassure the American people that it was just a temporary downturn in the economy. 'Prosperity is just around the corner', said Hoover.

What action did Hoover's government take?

Hoover and the Republicans believed it was not the government's role to interfere in the way business operated, or in people's lives. When the Depression set in, Hoover encouraged private charities and individual states to provide local help for those who were in need. However, as things became worse, the Republican government did act.

> The Hawley-Smoot Tariff, another tax on imports, was introduced in 1930. This did not help, however, as foreign countries raised their tariffs in retaliation. Consequently fewer American goods were sold abroad.

> Taxes were reduced to give the population more purchasing power. This was ineffective because many people were unemployed and had no income to pay less tax on.

> The Reconstruction Finance Corporation was set up to lend $2,000 million to banks, companies and state governments. This funded unemployment relief and public work projects and achieved some success under the next government.

Hoover was a talented and sincere president, who did care about ordinary Americans. However he lacked both vision and communication skills. He failed to show the American people that he was doing enough to solve the country's problems.

SOURCE A

This historian argues that Hoover was too rigid in his approach:

He was a good man, but he clung to the traditional American beliefs of individualism and laissez-faire. He continued to believe in private charity. However, the facts were that in Illinois, for example, the Red Cross could, by 1931, provide only 75 cents a week for hungry families. The situation had developed far beyond the ability of private charity to cope.

D. K. Adams, *FDR and the New Deal*, 1979

SOURCE B

By 1932, people had lost faith in Hoover's ability to solve the problems. By contrast, a two-mile-long parade greeted Roosevelt when he arrived at Indianapolis during the election campaign.

Franklin Roosevelt

Franklin Delano Roosevelt, the Democratic candidate for the 1932 election, seemed to many Americans to be cheerful, optimistic, and full of positive plans for recovery.

Born in 1882 in New York State, Roosevelt came from a very privileged and wealthy background. After leaving Harvard he eventually became a Democratic senator. During the First World War, he helped to run the US Navy as Assistant Secretary.

In 1921, at the age of 39, Roosevelt caught polio (poliomyelitis) and, for a time, was paralysed from the waist down. For several years, he struggled to get better and, with the help of steel leg braces and crutches, eventually managed to walk short distances.

By 1928, Roosevelt was ready to stand as a candidate for the governorship of New York State. After election, he raised $20 million in new taxes to provide food, clothing and shelter for the unemployed in New York.

What was Franklin Roosevelt offering the American people?

During the 1932 election campaign, Roosevelt said: 'I pledge you, I pledge myself, to a New Deal for the US people.' He spoke about the 'forgotten man at the bottom of the economic pyramid', and was shocked to see 'millions living in conditions labelled indecent half a century ago'. When he promised to take direct government action, many poorer Americans took comfort from his words.

To many middle-class voters in 1932, Roosevelt seemed to be a safer choice than Hoover. They felt that, if America really was on the brink of revolution, Roosevelt's policies might give unemployed people some hope, and draw them back from violence and despair.

SOURCE C

Roosevelt meets two farmers from Georgia in the course of his campaign.

SOURCE D

William Green, a trade union leader, said in 1931:

I warn the people who are exploiting the workers that they can only drive them so far before they will turn on them and destroy them. Revolution grows out of the depths of hunger.

Time Magazine, October 1931

In November 1932, 23 million people (57 per cent of those voting) gave Roosevelt their trust. Now he faced the enormous challenge of taking America out of the worst economic depression in its history.

>> Activity

Explain what were the main factors that enabled FDR to win the 1932 election.

The collapse of the American economy

THE WEAKNESSES IN THE AMERICAN ECONOMY

> Wealth was unevenly distributed. Only a small proportion of the population could afford to buy luxury items.

> It was difficult to sell American goods abroad. Foreign countries imposed high trade tariffs in retaliation against US import taxes.

> By the end of the 1920s, too many goods were being produced for the market.

> There was a huge build-up of debt, as many people bought on credit or hire purchase.

> The Wall Street share boom. Prices rose but were based on demand rather than on the real value of companies.

EFFECTS OF THE CRASH ON AMERICAN SOCIETY

> By 1933, 14 million people were out of work.

> By 1933, over 4,000 banks had gone out of business.

> Blacks and American farmers suffered especially severely.

> Hoovervilles grew up on the outskirts of cities.

> Protests came from farmers faced with evictions, and from the Bonus Army.

THE WALL STREET CRASH

24 October: Black Thursday: 13 million shares were sold. Prices plummeted. Huge losses were made. The banks called in loans.

25 October: Prices steadied but not for long. Bankers tried to restore confidence.

28 October: Prices fell again: 9 million shares were traded.

29 October: Terrifying Tuesday: 16 million shares were thrown on the market. $8,000 million was lost by shareholders.

13 November: The lowest level was reached. Total losses amounted to $30–40,000 million.

President Hoover

Hoover and the Republicans told Americans that 'Prosperity is just around the corner'. The government believed in a policy of laissez-faire. Eventually taxes were reduced, and tariffs were increased against foreign imports but this did little. The Republican Party and President Hoover were blamed by many Americans for the effects of the Crash. In 1932, it seemed that they were offering the American public 'more of the same'.

Franklin D. Roosevelt

Roosevelt was a complete contrast to President Hoover. He came from a wealthy background, but understood the problems of ordinary people affected by the Depression. Roosevelt said he was offering the American people a 'New Deal' that would involve direct government action, where necessary, to fight the Depression. The American people agreed, and, in November 1932, 23 million (57 per cent in all) voted for Roosevelt.

The principles behind the New Deal

In his opening speech as President, Roosevelt spoke these famous words:

'Let me first of all assert my firm belief that the only thing we have to fear is fear itself. Nameless, unreasoning, unjustified terror which paralyses efforts to convert retreat into advance. This is no insolvable problem. This nation asks for action and action now.'

Relief, recovery and reform

The New Deal was based on three themes or principles.

The first New Deal (1933) was based on relief and recovery. The relief was aimed at the homeless and unemployed of the Depression. The recovery was needed for industry and agriculture.

The second New Deal (1934–40) was based more on reform and measures to prevent such a depression from happening again.

Government involvement

After Roosevelt was sworn in as American President on 4 March 1933, the Democrats introduced policies that were very different from those of the Republicans. Numerous laws were drafted that would involve the Federal government in the affairs of the individual states and ordinary people as never before.

Although Roosevelt was not working to any particular economic theory, the one essential element in the New Deal was direct government action. This was why it was so different from the previous policies of the Republican governments.

The New Deal has been compared by some historians to the theories of a British economist, J. M. Keynes. He suggested that, in order to get out of depression, governments should:

> take positive action to get things moving by increasing spending on public works, thus creating new jobs

> by this means give money back to people to 'prime the pump' and get them spending again, creating new hope

> give grants and cheap loans to help businesses.

Many of Roosevelt's critics said that his policies, like those recommended by Keynes, meant too much interference in business and the lives of individuals.

'Action and action now'

Roosevelt had also said in his inaugural speech that he would be asking Congress for emergency powers. He used an Act from the First World War, the Trading with the Enemy Act, that allowed him to take extraordinary action to deal with the crisis. His first priority was to put the banks on a secure footing.

Roosevelt makes his first speech to the nation as President.

Solving the bank crisis

President Roosevelt realised that he had to restore faith in the capitalist business system. If the USA were to make a recovery, then he had to encourage people to invest in industry once more. Before this could happen, the banks had to be seen to be stable. By 1933, 4,000 banks had collapsed. About 15 per cent of people's life savings had been lost. Millions of Americans had withdrawn their money, and overseas investors had removed most of their gold deposits.

The Emergency Banking Act

Just two days after his inauguration, on 6 March, the President ordered all banks to shut for a four-day Bank Holiday. He then asked Congress to pass the Emergency Banking Act. This would allow government officials to inspect the accounts of every bank in America. Only those with adequate cash reserves and those that were properly managed would be allowed to re-open. Savers' money would be guaranteed by the government. (This was further reinforced by the 1935 Banking Act, which increased government control over banks.)

The Act was passed by Congress, and on Sunday 12 March, President Roosevelt gave his first 'fireside chat' to the nation. He started by saying: 'I want to talk for a few minutes to the American people about banking.' He then went on:

> 'Some of our bankers have shown themselves either incompetent or dishonest in their handling of people's funds. It is the government's job to straighten out this situation and do it as quickly as possible. We must have faith; you must not be stampeded by rumours. Together we cannot fail.'

The effect was dramatic. On Monday 13 March, the banks re-opened, and the panic had stopped. Gold deposits worth $300 million returned and confidence was restored in the banking system. Gradually, ordinary people began to return their money to the banks.

Discussion point

> Why would the Republicans criticise Roosevelt and the Democrats for their reform policies?

Roosevelt facing the microphones as he makes his fourteenth fireside chat from the White House. Roosevelt realised the impact he could make by speaking to the whole nation by radio.

The New Deal in 1933

The 'First 100 Days', the period from 9 March 1933 to 6 June 1933, is a unique period in American history. President Roosevelt and his team drafted an extraordinary number of new laws, all of which were passed by Congress.

What was so different about the New Deal?

SOURCE A

A junior member of Roosevelt's government remembers the 100 days:

They were exciting, exhilarating days. It was one of the most joyous periods of my life. We were infected with a spirit of adventure, for something concrete and constructive was finally being done about the chaos.

T. L. Stokes, *Chip off my Shoulder,* 1940

SOURCE B

A poster showing the American economy being lifted out of depression.

Cutting government spending

Roosevelt kept to one of his election promises by passing the Economy Act on 15 March. This Act reduced government expenditure by cutting the pay of all government employees and members of the armed forces by 15 per cent. Government departments had their budgets cut by up to 25 per cent.

The ending of Prohibition

The Democrat government decided to lift Prohibition as a matter of urgency. On 20 March, the Beer Act was passed, making the manufacture and sale of beer legal again. This not only brought in extra tax revenue to the government but reduced one of the main sources of income for organised crime.

Agricultural Adjustment Act (AAA)

This Act reduced and controlled farm production, causing prices to rise. The AAA paid farmers to produce less. In 1933, for instance, 6 million piglets were destroyed – but the meat was canned and given to the unemployed.

Between 1932 and 1939, the income of farmers more than doubled. Many people criticised the Act, saying that this was unjustified government interference in the free market.

SOURCE C

A joke of the 1930s:

Socialism – You own two cows, give one to your neighbour;

Communism – Give both cows to the government and the government gives you back some milk;

Fascism – Keep the cows but give the milk to the government, which sells some back to you;

New Dealism – Shoot both cows and milk the government.

Civilian Conservation Corps (CCC)

This was set up to provide work for unemployed 18–25 year-old men on conservation schemes. The CCC provided camps for the men to stay in, while they cut fire breaks through forests, planted trees, and became involved with many conservation tasks. They were paid $30 a month and had to send home $25. Over 9 years, 2 million young men benefited from the work.

The CCC was compared by some critics to the Hitler Youth movement. Trade union leaders too, were unsure about its value, suggesting that it exploited young workers.

Civil Works Administration (CWA)

This organisation provided public works jobs for the unemployed.

It was a short-term measure that provided minimum pay. Within a few months, work had been found for 4 million people on a variety of projects that included building new dams, roads, schools, public buildings and toilets.

Many, however, felt that they were working on useless jobs, called 'boondoggles'.

SOURCE D

SOURCE E

A member of the government comments on the scheme:

They set up this CWA very hurriedly. No means test – any guy could just walk into the county office and get a job. Leaf raking, cleaning up libraries, painting the town hall – within 60 days, 4 million were put to work.

C. B. Baldwin, Assistant to Secretary of Agriculture

SOURCE F

One member of the CCC said when interviewed in Chicago:

I was at a CCC camp for 6 months, came home for 15 months, looked for work, and I couldn't make $30 a month, so I enlisted back in CCCs and went to Michigan. Spent 6 months planting trees. Came out – still no money to be made. So back in CCCs. Spent $4\frac{1}{2}$ months fighting forest fires.

Blackie Gold, late 1930s

SOURCE G

A historian writes of the value of the CCCs:

They planted trees, made reservoirs, raised bridges, protected and improved parks, forests. They came from large cities, small towns, slum street corners. Their muscles hardened, self-respect returned. More important, they learned about America and about other Americans.

A. Schlesinger, *Coming of the New Deal*, 1959

Federal Emergency Relief Administration (FERA)

FERA had two functions: to provide emergency cash relief for the poor and to give help to the poor relief schemes set up by individual states. It gave $500 million in all to state governments for this purpose. As the money was given, not lent, it seemed wrong to many Americans.

President Roosevelt and his officials visit the CCC Camp in Virginia's Shenandoah Valley in 1933.

Home Owners' Loan Corporation (HOLC)

The HOLC gave help to home owners desperate to keep up mortgage payments so that they would not lose their homes. These loans were made with low interest rates.

National Industrial Recovery Act (NIRA)

The target of NIRA was to provide jobs and to stimulate the economy.

NIRA consisted of two parts, the Public Works Administration (PWA) and the National Recovery Administration (NRA).

The Public Works Administration

Like the CWA, the PWA created jobs for unemployed men on building houses, roads, bridges and public buildings.

The National Recovery Administration

This was an organisation that encouraged companies to provide good conditions for their workers and recognise trade unions, while still making reasonable profits. Companies were encouraged to sign NRA codes that fixed fair prices and minimum wages.

In return for signing the codes, a company received a Blue Eagle badge. This was a logo that the company could use in selling its products.

SOURCE H

A PWA building project.

SOURCE I

The NRA Blue Eagle symbol.

By September 1933, over 5,000 industries, employing 22 million workers, had signed up.

There were criticisms and problems. Many employers were totally against the idea of trade unions. Some, like Henry Ford, refused to sign any codes. Many workers were very disappointed by these attitudes, and went on strike.

It was also suggested that many industries used the NRA to push up prices.

SOURCE J

Roosevelt's view of the NRA:

In my inaugural, I laid down the proposition that nobody is going to starve in this country. It seems to me equally plain that no business which depends for its existence on paying less than living wages has any right to continue in this country.

President Roosevelt, 1933

>> Activity

1 How did the new agencies improve the lives of ordinary Americans?

2 Which laws were designed to get industry moving and people back to work?

3 What were the most common criticisms of the New Deal agencies of 1933?

The New Deal and the farmers

In April 1933, in the mid-West state of Iowa, 500 farmers seized and almost lynched Judge Bradley, who was signing eviction orders. This act of desperation clearly showed the growing anger among poor farmers. For many, their income was just one-third of what it had been in 1929.

What was done to solve the problems of the farming industry?

Okies and Arkies

In the Mid-West of America, poor farming methods meant that the land could be easily eroded by wind. From 1933 to 1934, there was a long drought following what had been a scorching summer. The land was turned into a huge 'dust bowl' of light, sandy earth. When the autumn winds came they blew the soil away. The terrible dust storms that resulted brought ordinary life to a standstill. Schools and factories closed and cars and lorries were buried under drifts of dust.

SOURCE A

YEARS OF DUS

A poster issued in 1935 highlighting the terrible consequences of the dust storms.

Many thousands of farms were destroyed by the dust storms, particularly in the states of Oklahoma and Arkansas. Over 350,000 so-called Okies and Arkies loaded their belongings onto their trucks or cars and moved towards the richer farming states in the west like California and Oregon.

THE AREAS AFFECTED BY THE DUST STORMS

Life was desperately hard for the migrants who often received little sympathy from their new neighbours. Many believed that they were responsible for their own problems.

SOURCE B

The impact of a dust storm is like a shovel full of fine sand flung against the face ... Cars come to a standstill, for no light in the world can penetrate that swirling muck.

New Republic Magazine, 1935

SOURCE C

This historian reflects on the animosity towards the migrants:

Some conservatives claimed that relief women had babies to qualify for higher payments. Even the FERA investigator, Martha Gelhorn, wrote in 1934: 'It is accepted that the more incapable the parents, the more offspring they produce'.

R. S. McElvaine, *The Great Depression*, 1984

Roosevelt saw help for the farmers as a top priority. He introduced a farming programme which meant that things improved for most farmers. The prices of farm produce rose and, by 1939, farmers' incomes had doubled since 1932. It is not surprising that President Roosevelt was strongly supported by millions of farmers, helping him to gain re-election in 1936, 1940 and 1944.

ROOSEVELT'S FARMING PROGRAMME

> The Agricultural Adjustment Act (AAA) was passed in the First 100 Days to control production and raise prices (see page 47).

> The Farm Credit Administration (FCA) re-financed 20 per cent of farmers' mortgages.

> The Farm Security Administration (FSA) helped evicted sharecroppers (tenant farmers who work the land in return for a share of the produce) find homes and loans.

> The Tennessee Valley Authority (TVA) provided help and work for thousands over a vast area.

SOURCE D

A novelist describes the plight of the people the farming programme was intended to help:

The cars of the migrant people crawled out of the side roads onto the great cross-country highway, and they scuttled like bugs to the westward ... they were lonely and perplexed ... they huddled together; they talked together; they shared their lives, their food, and the things they hoped for in the new country.

John Steinbeck, *The Grapes of Wrath*, 1939

SOURCE E

A migrant agricultural worker's family, California, March 1936. The FSA hired a team of photographers whose work became world famous. Among them were Dorothea Lange and Walker Evans. Their pictures of the suffering of the poorest Americans during the Great Depression became well known. The photograph shown here is one of those taken by Dorothea Lange. It shows vividly the despair and suffering that could be seen on the faces of people like these.

The Tennessee Valley Authority (TVA)

This authority was set up to improve and develop a poor region across seven states for the benefit of the community, to develop industry, and to provide jobs for thousands of workers.

The Tennessee Valley was a vast agricultural area as large as England and Wales. Intensive farming of the land had led to soil erosion, dust damage and flooding. The Tennessee River flooded every spring, washing away topsoil, and, in summer, the land became dry and difficult to cultivate. It was an area with very little industry and high unemployment. President Roosevelt decided that improving this area was a priority. He set up the TVA, which proved to be a massive undertaking. It became the most notable achievement of the New Deal.

THE AREA COVERED BY THE TENNESSEE VALLEY AUTHORITY

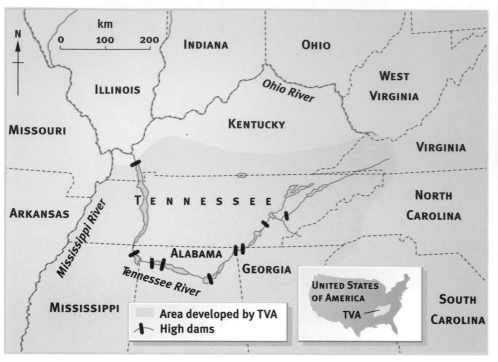

SOURCE G

The Watts Bar Dam being constructed on the Tennessee River.

SOURCE F

One writer said:

The TVA brought new ideas, new wealth, new skills, new hope into a wasted, tired and discouraged region.

Carl Degler, *Out of the Past*, 1959

THE ACHIEVEMENTS OF THE TVA

> Dams were built to control the Tennessee River and produce electricity. By 1940, 21 dams provided waterpower to produce 3,200 million kilowatts of electricity each year.

> New lakes were created, new locks built and 1000 kilometres of the river opened up for navigation. Materials could now be brought in and produce taken out.

> Power stations were constructed to provide cheap electricity for homes, farms and factories.

> Farmers were shown how to regenerate the land by using fertilisers.

> Farmers were encouraged to prevent soil erosion by planting thousands of trees.

> Many new jobs were created.

Criticisms of the TVA

Roosevelt's opponents claimed that the Federal government should not interfere in the problems of individual states. Private companies should have done the work. It was unlikely, however, that private companies would have been willing to take such a risk.

>> Activity

1 Explain how farmers' lives were made worse by the Great Depression.

2 Did Roosevelt really provide positive help for American farmers? Give evidence to support your answer.

3 What were Roosevelt's critics likely to have said about his farming policy?

The New Deal 1934–40

After 1933, the New Deal legislation began to concentrate more on issues of reform rather than relief and recovery.

How did the New Deal change after 1933?

Roosevelt's aims after 1933

Roosevelt now turned his attention to social reform in order to provide security for those affected by the Depression. He also wanted to give more protection to the working population and to replace the agencies ruled illegal by the Supreme Court (see page 56).

Works Progress Administration (WPA), 1934

The WPA, a big new public works agency, was set up to put people to work on projects valuable to the community. This agency took over the work of the CWA and the PWA, and was run by Harry Hopkins. By 1937, 11,000 schools and public buildings had been completed and 69,000 kilometres (43,000 miles) of roads had been built.

Employment was also given to workers in other areas. Unemployed writers were asked to produce guide books to states and cities. Artists painted murals and actors were sent out on nationwide tours. The WPA gave work to 2 million people a year between 1935 and 1941.

Securities and Exchange Commission, 1934

The Securities and Exchange Commission was set up to prevent another 'Wall Street Crash'. It regulated the conduct of the Stock Exchange and the way in which stocks and shares were offered for sale. People now had to make a minimum down-payment of 50–60 per cent of the cost before buying shares.

National Labor Relations Act 1935

The National Labor Relations Act (the Wagner Act) replaced NIRA.

It was a charter for the workers. This Act gave workers the right to form and join trade unions. Employers could not penalise those workers who did so. The National Labor Relations Board was set up to protect the rights of workers.

TRADE UNION MEMBERSHIP, 1933–9

1933	3 million
1937	4 million
1938	7 million
1939	9 million

SOURCE A

The WPA in Kentucky, in 1937. A truck is being loaded with flood debris.

Trade unions and industrial unrest

In 1936, the miners' leader, John Lewis, brought together many separate unions into one big organisation called the Congress of Industrial Organisations (CIO). Union membership increased. Many joined the new CIO, others joined the older American Federation of Labor.

Some big companies refused to let their workers join a union. Men were hired to break up workers' meetings and strikes.

In 1937, sit-down strikes in the car and steel industries were followed by all-out strikes involving violent clashes between strikers and police.

SOURCE B

Some companies were very aggressive towards workers who tried to form a union, for example the Henry Ford Organisation:

There are about 800 underworld characters in the Ford organisation: the storm troops (or goon squads). They keep order through terror. Around this nucleus, there are between 8,000 and 9,000 spies and informers – the fear in the plant is something indescribable. Workers seen talking together are fired.

From an official inquiry in the state of Connecticut, 1932

SOURCE C

The end of the sit-down strike at General Motors in November 1937.

Social Security Act (SSA) 1935

The Social Security Act has been called the 'most far reaching piece of social legislation in US history'. It was really several laws in one, and provided for:

> pensions for the old and widows of up to $85 a month

> help for the disabled and children in need

> a national system of insurance for the unemployed.

Never before had the government taken direct action to help the poor.

SOURCE D

This is what one modern historian says about criticism of the Social Security Act:

With plans to collect so much money and give it to so few people, the social security programme became a natural target for the President's rivals. Alf Landon, the 1936 Republican [presidential] candidate, described the SS Act as 'unjust, unworkable, and wastefully financed'.

Ed Berkowitz, *America's Welfare State*, 1991

Soil Conservation Act 1936

The Soil Conservation Act replaced the AAA, which had been ruled illegal by the Supreme Court. It made grants to farmers who improved and conserved the soil on their lands.

Fair Labor Standards Act 1938

The Fair Labor Standards Act built on the Wagner Act of 1935. It established maximum hours of work and minimum wages. It also controlled the use of child labour: no one under the age of 16 was to work full-time.

>> Activity

1 How did the nature of the New Deal change after 1933?

2 What were the main features of the new laws and agencies introduced from 1934 on?

3 How did each one affect the lives of ordinary American citizens?

The enemies of the New Deal

President Roosevelt and his government faced many enemies. Many criticisms of the New Deal were made because of the fact that the Federal government now interfered more in people's lives.

MAIN CRITICISMS OF THE NEW DEAL

1. The government was spending huge sums of public money on unnecessary projects and works.

2. The New Deal was an attack on 'free institutions', and interfered too much with business and industry.

3. The New Deal destroyed people's initiative: welfare was bad for a man's spirit.

4. The Federal government was becoming too powerful, and was taking over in areas that should be the responsibility of individual states. The President had too much power.

Opposition from the right

Businessmen and conservatives

Many business leaders and industrialists said that the New Deal interfered with their freedom to manage their business in the way they wanted. They disliked the NRA, and felt that trade unions were becoming too powerful.

A cartoon from Punch *defending Roosevelt from accusations that he was too revolutionary.*

The rich and privileged

Many of the wealthy resented Roosevelt. They saw him as a threat to their privilege and power and disliked the extra taxes that had been imposed on them.

The press barons and newspaper owners

All the powerful and conservative owners of the big newspapers were enemies of Roosevelt and the New Deal. They attacked him for being a socialist, and even a communist.

Opposition from the left

Socialists and communists attacked the New Deal because they felt that it did not do enough to help the poor and underprivileged. Although trade unions had more status, workers in many industries were still paid low wages.

Huey Long: the 'Kingfish'

Huey Long strongly opposed the New Deal. As Governor of Louisiana, he brought in socialist measures providing relief and help for the poor. He used public money for roads, hospitals and schools.

Long embarked on a 'Share our Wealth' campaign which proposed the following:

> all fortunes over $3 million to be confiscated

> every US family to get $4,000 to buy a home, car and radio

> free education for all Americans

> a national minimum wage

> old age pensions and cheap food for the poor.

These ideas may have seemed reasonable to many poor Americans. In fact, Long was a crook who got rid of opponents, rigged elections, and bribed the police. He was always protected by a group of bodyguards. Unfortunately for Long, they could not prevent him being shot by an assassin in 1935.

Father Charles Coughlin

Coughlin was a Roman Catholic priest who ran a radio programme that attracted a large audience. In 1935, he set up the National Union for Social Justice to provide work and fair wages for everyone. He said that Roosevelt was 'anti-God', and stood as a candidate in the 1936 presidential election.

Roosevelt and the Supreme Court

Perhaps the most serious threat to the New Deal programme came from the US Supreme Court. The nine judges of the Supreme Court can decide whether laws passed by Congress are 'in harmony with the constitution'. If they decide that a law is not, they can veto that particular law.

In 1935, the Schechter Poultry Group broke one of the NRA codes by selling diseased chickens. The NRA took the company to court and the Schechter company was found guilty. The company appealed against the decision and the Supreme Court upheld their appeal, ruling that the NRA had no right to interfere in state affairs, in this case, the New York poultry trade. The NRA code was declared illegal.

Consequently, all the other 750 NRA codes were now also illegal. The Supreme Court went on to rule the AAA illegal, and another 11 Alphabet Agencies (so called because they were always known by their initials) were also declared 'unconstitutional'.

What was President Roosevelt's reaction?

Roosevelt was very angry. As he saw it, the Alphabet Agencies were all involved in solving national problems. He also felt that his New Deal policies were making revolution less likely.

In 1937, he presented a Bill to Congress that would allow the President to replace any judges over the age of 70 who had served

Huey Long drives home a point as he is interviewed by reporters in 1933.

ten years. As five judges were in their 70s, and one was 80, this would have removed six at a stroke. In the event, Congress believed that the President was trying to alter the Constitution and refused to pass the Bill.

Roosevelt the dictator?

From 1937, the Supreme Court judges no longer opposed the New Deal legislation. In any case, as they reached retirement age, President Roosevelt replaced them with people of his own choosing. The Supreme Court dispute caused a lot of Americans to lose faith in Roosevelt and his political judgement. Many felt that he was acting like a dictator.

The 1936 Presidential election

President Roosevelt once said: 'Everyone's agin me except the voters!' He was right. When the votes were counted, it was clear that Roosevelt and the Democrats had won a landslide victory. Out of 48 states, 46 had voted for the New Deal.

President Roosevelt said, at a rally in Madison Square Gardens, in 1936, 'Of course, we will continue our efforts for the crippled, the blind, our insurance for the unemployed, our security for the aged.'

VOTING IN THE 1936, 1940 AND 1944 ELECTIONS

Year	Votes for Republicans	Votes for Democrats
1936	16,697,583	24,751,597
1940	22,304,755	27,243,466
1944	22,006,278	25,602,505

A new depression?

By 1937, the New Deal programmes had provided work for many, but there were still 7.7 million people out of work. President Roosevelt was concerned about increasing debt, and believed that the government should now give more responsibility back to individual states to solve their own problems. During the summer of 1937, overall government expenditure was cut and the large number of workers employed by the WPA was reduced.

World trade began to contract. The economy went into decline and unemployment soared. By 1938, almost 11 million people were out of work. It was feared that a new slump was beginning.

The government response was swift. Roosevelt asked Congress for $25,000 million to fund new PWA and WPA work schemes. By 1939, the economy seemed to be reviving once again but it is impossible to judge whether this improvement would have continued.

In September 1939, the Second World War broke out in Europe. From 1941 to 1945, American troops fought in Europe, in North Africa and the Pacific. Old factories had to be adapted and new ones built to supply all the weapons and equipment needed. The Americans, unemployed throughout the Depression years, were back at work again.

Discussion points

Look back to the information box listing the main criticisms of the New Deal on page 55.

> Who were the real enemies of the New Deal? Explain which of the criticisms would have been made by each opponent.

> Why were the opponents of the New Deal unable to stop the new laws?

THE TROJAN HORSE AT OUR GATE

AMERICAN CITIZENS

SCH!

CONSTITUTION OF THE UNITED STATES

NEW DEAL TYRANNY

NATIONAL RECOVERY

DEPRESSION

THE ILLEGAL ACT.
PRESIDENT ROOSEVELT. "I'M SORRY, BUT THE SUPREME COURT SAYS I MUST CHUCK YOU BACK AGAIN."

Two cartoons presenting different views of the New Deal.

Franklin Delano Roosevelt – the individual

On 13 April 1945, the day after Roosevelt's death, the Japanese Radio announced that it 'honoured the passing of a great man'. This was an extraordinary tribute from a sworn enemy of the United States.

How important a part did Franklin D. Roosevelt play in the success of the New Deal?

Many sources tell us about the popularity of Roosevelt the man.

SOURCE A

From a letter received at the White House in 1934:

Dear Mr President,

This is just to tell you everything is alright now. The man you sent found our house all right and we went down the bank with him and the mortgage can go on a while longer. You remember I wrote you about losing the furniture too. Well, your man got it back for us. I never heard of a President like you, Mr Roosevelt. Mrs — and I are old folks and don't amount to much, but we are joined with those millions of others in praying for you every night. God bless you, Mr Roosevelt.

SOURCE B

Roosevelt was popular with many Americans, even journalists, as this photograph shows.

SOURCE C

A historian writes:

A whole generation grew up knowing no other presidential style than stability, courage and a joyful optimism.

The fireside chats brought him into millions of living rooms – even his audible sipping of water endeared him to the US people: 'My friends, it is very hot here in Washington tonight'.

President Roosevelt had the utter conviction that it was people that counted.

S. G. Spackman, 'Roosevelt', in *History Today*, 1983

SOURCE D

A modern historian expresses the opinion that Roosevelt was either loved or hated by American people:

It is possible to describe him as both the most popular and least popular president this century. That is, a greater number of Americans revered him more than any other president, and a greater number loathed and despised him!

Esmund Wright, *The American Dream*, 1996

>> Activity

Look at Sources A–D. What evidence can you find to support the following statement:

'Roosevelt had a particular personality and charm which enabled him to attract the support of millions of American people.'

An assessment of the New Deal

Historians have written many studies of the New Deal and have come to many different conclusions about its success.

How successful was the New Deal?

THREE INTERPRETATIONS OF THE NEW DEAL

Interpretation A

The New Deal was a total success. Roosevelt and the Democrats were able to put Americans back to work, get industry moving again, and drag their country out of the Depression. Workers received protection through trade unions, and millions found work through the Alphabet Agencies. Roosevelt achieved these things by democratic means.

Interpretation B

The New Deal failed to bring America out of the Depression. In 1938, unemployment was back up to almost 11 million. The government spent huge sums of money on wasteful schemes, and interfered in industry and people's lives. In some cases, President Roosevelt acted like a dictator, for example over the Supreme Court issue.

Interpretation C

The New Deal was a partial success. Although it did not completely solve the problems of the Depression, it gave millions of Americans the will to carry on. However, the number of jobless rose again, in 1938, to 11 million. It was only the Second World War that finally reduced unemployment in America.

Negative interpretations of the New Deal

SOURCE A

Those who feared that Franklin Roosevelt was being a dictator said that the New Deal was illegal, unconstitutional and dictatorial. They objected strongly to his taxes and other proposals that tended to redistribute wealth.

David Fromkin, *In the Time of the Americans*, 1996

SOURCE B

Politically, Roosevelt suffered a staggering setback from his fight with the Supreme Court. He appeared to his opponents and even to a considerable part of the public to be like a dictator.

Frank Freidel, *Franklin D. Roosevelt: A Rendezvous with Destiny,* 1990

SOURCE C

Critics of Franklin D. Roosevelt's administrative methods (they were and are numerous) point in scorn to the fact that the programme changed its form almost yearly – or more often!

D. W. Brogan, *Penguin History of USA,* 1985

SOURCE D

Every survey of American historians finds Franklin Roosevelt ranked as one of this nation's greatest presidents – that he was the right choice to lead the USA through the midst of the Great Depression. Only careful reading reveals that despite Roosevelt's immense labours to feed the unemployed, only modest recovery was attained before the outbreak of World War Two. There is, in short, much about Roosevelt and the New Deal that historians need to re-evaluate.

Gary D. Beast, *Pride, Prejudice and Politics: Roosevelt versus Recovery,* 1991

SOURCE E

The unemployed queue in front of a 1936 hoarding, designed to restore confidence to the economy.

Positive interpretations of the New Deal

SOURCE F

On balance, the New Deal had an immense constructive impact. By 1939, the country was committed to the idea that the federal government should accept responsibility for national welfare ...'Never again', the Republican presidential candidate was to say in 1952, 'shall we allow a depression in the United States.'

J. A. Garraty, *Short History of the United States*, 1985

SOURCE G

I do not believe that the real essence of Roosevelt's achievement is in the federal agencies. It is derived from the combined impact of his domestic reforms. In the truest possible sense, Roosevelt included the excluded.

Joseph Alsop, *Franklin Roosevelt, 1882–1945: A Century Remembered*, 1982

SOURCE H

By 1939, the farmer's income was twice that of 1932. The National Recovery Act had shortened working hours and raised wages. The WPA found new building projects. The federal government even brought in social security benefits for the unemployed and old. These measures set the country on the road to recovery, and they were not socialist. His job, as he saw it, was to revive the capitalist system. He had to inspire in Americans a new faith in themselves. He was successful.

Esmund Wright, *The American Dream*, 1996

SOURCE I

Roosevelt's importance lay in his ability to arouse the country, and the men who served under him, by his breezy encouragement of experimentation, by his hopefulness and his idealism.

William Leuchtenburg, *Franklin D. Roosevelt and the New Deal*, 1963

SOURCE J

President Roosevelt signing the Social Security Act on 14 August 1935.

SOURCE K

Finally, a mixed view from a recent book about Roosevelt:

The New Deal was at best a half success. But, FDR restored US faith in itself and its institutions; developed a managed economy and launched a welfare state. Intellectuals may scoff at the disorderliness of his thought processes, but democracy is at least as much a matter of the heart as of the head.

Michael Simpson, *Franklin D. Roosevelt*, 1989

>> Activity

1 Look at the views of the New Deal in Sources A–K.

2 Using your knowledge of the New Deal, explain whether you agree with any of the three interpretations on page 59.

America and the Second World War

Throughout the 1920s and 1930s, the United States of America had followed an isolationist policy with respect to the rest of the world. President Roosevelt, however, warned Congress that America could not continue to ignore the problems in Europe.

Why did America enter the Second World War?

The rise of the dictators

During the 1930s, many European countries came under the control of right-wing fascist dictators. Nazi Germany, under Adolf Hitler, began to act aggressively to neighbouring states throughout Europe. In 1935, the Italians, under Mussolini, invaded Abyssinia (now Ethiopia) in the Horn of Africa. General Franco, the leader of the Spanish fascists, won a Civil War in Spain against the communists. Japan invaded China.

Cash and Carry

After Hitler invaded Poland in September 1939, Britain and France had declared war on Nazi Germany. The US Congress was persuaded to change the Neutrality Laws and set up the Cash and Carry plan. Under this scheme, Britain and France could buy military supplies from the United States as long as they transported them from America in British or French ships.

The fall of France

In June 1940, France was overrun by the Germans, and the British Army was defeated at Dunkirk. Britain stood alone against Nazi Germany. Roosevelt was determined that America would provide every piece of military equipment she could: guns, ammunition, artillery and heavy weaponry. Britain was short of money due to the cost of fighting the war. The Prime Minister of Britain, Winston Churchill, pleaded with the Americans: 'Give us the tools – we will finish the job.'

The Lend-Lease Scheme

Roosevelt's solution was to draw up an agreement that would allow America to lend military equipment to Britain free of charge. Despite some protests in America, Congress agreed. In March 1941, a Bill was passed to allow for the loan of war materials to any country whose defence was necessary for American safety. Guns, ships and food started pouring into Britain.

SOURCE A

The first group of American destroyers under the Lend-Lease Scheme arrive in a British port.

61

The Atlantic Charter

To cement the alliance between America and Britain, Churchill and Roosevelt arranged a historic meeting in August 1941. They met aboard an American cruiser, USS *Augusta,* in the mid-Atlantic. At this meeting, they agreed to work together for international peace after the war.

SOURCE B

This was President Roosevelt's statement at the end of the Charter. He named four essential freedoms for mankind:

The allies deem it right to make known certain common principles in the national policies of their countries, on which they base their hopes for a better future

1 Freedom of speech and expression

2 Freedom of worship

3 Freedom from want

4 Freedom from fear.

SOURCE C

Roosevelt and Churchill on board HMS The Prince of Wales, *in August 1941, during the Atlantic Charter Conference. Both leaders had great respect and liking for each other.*

America enters the war

Relations between America and Japan had worsened in the late 1930s.

In July 1937, Japan invaded China and after the collapse of France, Japan also occupied French Indo-China. This resulted in Roosevelt freezing all Japanese money and assets in the USA.

On 7 December 1941, Japanese carrier-borne aircraft carried out a dawn attack on the US Pacific fleet at anchor in Pearl Harbor. They sank eight battleships and killed over 2,000 US military personnel. President Roosevelt called it 'a day which will live in infamy'.

On 8 December, Congress declared war on Japan. Three days later, Italy and Germany declared war on America.

SOURCE D

A small boat rescues a seaman from the water near the blazing USS West Virginia. *It rests on the bottom after it was hit by Japanese bombs and torpedoes during the attack on Pearl Harbor.*

>> Activity

1 How did President Roosevelt help Britain before the USA went to war?

2 Why did the USA finally enter the Second World War?

The New Deal in action

THE NEW DEAL

> Relief: practical help was urgently needed for the homeless and unemployed.

> Recovery: action was urgently needed to revitalise industry and agriculture.

> Reform: changes were needed to prevent such a depression happening again.

Roosevelt was determined to use Federal government money to achieve this.

SOLVING THE BANKING CRISIS

> The Trading with the Enemy Act was used to grant President Roosevelt emergency powers.

> All banks were closed for four days from 6 March 1933.

> The Emergency Banking Act was passed.

> The banks re-opened on 13 March. Confidence was restored.

THE FARMING PROGRAMME

> The Agricultural Adjustment Act (AAA) was passed.

> The Farm Credit Administration (FCA) provided mortgages to help farmers.

> The Farm Security Administration (FSA) gave help to evicted sharecroppers.

> The Tennessee Valley Authority (TVA) improved living conditions in seven states where land was infertile and eroded. It built dams to prevent flooding and produce electricity. It provided employment for thousands and showed farmers how to regenerate the land.

THE FIRST 100 DAYS OF ACTIVITY: MARCH–JUNE 1933

> The Economy Act reduced government spending.

> The Beer Act ended Prohibition.

> The Agricultural Adjustment Act (AAA) provided loans and advisers for farmers.

> The Civilian Conservation Corps (CCC) gave work to young men, on conservation tasks.

> The Civil Works Administration (CWA) provided public work tasks for 4 million people.

> The Federal Emergency Relief Administration (FERA) gave immediate cash help to the poor.

> The National Industrial Recovery Act (NIRA) set up the Public Works Administration (PWA), which created jobs on public building schemes, and the National Recovery Administration (NRA). The NRA encouraged businesses to achieve a 'Blue Eagle' badge.

NEW DEAL 1934–40

The emphasis now shifted from relief and recovery to reform. Major new laws and agencies were created.

> The Works Progress Administration (WPA) took over the work of the CWA and PWA, and aimed to provide work valuable to the community. It provided jobs for 2 million people each year.

> The Securities and Exchange Commission was set up to regulate the work of the Stock Exchange.

> The National Labor Relations Act (Wagner Act) replaced NIRA, giving workers the right to join unions. The National Relations Labor Board was set up to protect workers.

> The Social Security Act was passed providing for the first-ever relief and welfare payments for the poor and unemployed.

There was a second depression in 1937–8, but the economy revived again after further Federal government spending.

THE ENEMIES OF THE NEW DEAL

> Businessmen and press barons criticised Roosevelt for interfering with the freedom of business and industry.

> The rich and privileged saw President Roosevelt as a threat to their position and wealth, and disliked the higher taxes imposed on them.

> Socialists and communists complained that Roosevelt's government had not changed the basic structure of society – the owners of industry still had all the power and wages were still low.

> The Supreme Court ruled that several Alphabet Agencies, including the NRA and AAA, were illegal because the Federal government was interfering in state affairs. The judges stopped their opposition after 1937.

WAS THE NEW DEAL A SUCCESS?

Strengths of the New Deal

> The economy began to recover.

> Unemployment was reduced from the 1932 level.

> Workers were given protection through trade unions.

> The principle of welfare and social security was established.

> The American people were given renewed faith and hope in their country.

> The New Deal saved the USA from the threat of revolution and dictatorship.

> There was some redistribution of wealth and power throughout American society.

Weaknesses of the New Deal

> In 1938–9, the unemployment figures rose to almost 11 million. It was the Second World War that finally put Americans back to work.

> There was great opposition to the principle of Federal government interference. Many businesses would not co-operate.

> Many huge corporations still had immense power, despite the New Deal.

> Support for trade unions caused great industrial unrest.

Roosevelt in 1937.

America and the Second World War

America had remained isolationist during the 1920s and 1930s, but Roosevelt persuaded Congress that the menace of Hitler and the Nazis could not be ignored.

The Cash and Carry Act of 1940 allowed Britain and France to buy and collect weapons from the USA. Under the Lend-Lease Act of 1941 the USA lent military equipment to Britain free of charge.

In August 1941, the Atlantic Charter was signed between the USA and Britain to work for peace after the Second World War.

After the Japanese bombed Pearl Harbor in December 1941, America declared war against Japan. Three days later, Germany and Italy declared war against America. America's part in the war was vital. American industry was harnessed to supply all the weapons and equipment needed. By 1945, unemployment was down to under 1 million.